AGENDA FOR SOCIAL JUSTICE: SOLUTIONS 2012

Glenn W. Muschert, Kathleen Ferraro,

Brian V. Klocke, Robert Perrucci,

and Jon Shefner (editors)

A Publication of the Justice 21 Committee

of the Society for the Study of Social Problems (SSSP)

Knoxville, Tennessee

Justice 21 Committee: Glenn W. Muschert (Chair), Miami University; Kathleen Ferraro, Northern Arizona University; Brian V. Klocke, State University of New York, Plattsburgh; JoAnn Miller, Purdue University; Robert Perrucci, Purdue University; Jon Shefner, University of Tennessee.

Marketing Associate: Jinjie (JJ) Chen.
Design Consultant: Helen Armstrong.
Cover Design: Helen Armstrong.
Organizational and Moral Support: Michele Koontz and Sharon Shumaker.
Production Support: Lisa East.
Web Mistress: Lisa East.
Typesetting: Glenn W. Muschert.

Volume Editors, Copy Editors, Proofreaders: Glenn W. Muschert, Kathleen Ferraro, Brian V. Klocke, Robert Perrucci, Jon Shefner.

This volume is available in Kindle format and Print format via Amazon.com.

Glenn W. Muschert, Kathleen Ferraro, Brian V. Klocke, Robert Perrucci, Jon Shefner (2012-08-01). Agenda for Social Justice: Solutions 2012. Society for the Study of Social Problems (US), Print Edition.

Library of Congress Cataloging-in-Publication Data
Agenda for social justice: solutions 2012 / Glenn W. Muschert, Kathleen Ferraro, Brian V. Klocke, Robert Perrucci, Jon Shefner. I. Title.

Printed in the United States of America
First Printing August 2012
ISBN-13: 978-1478397816
ISBN-10: 1478397810

CONTENTS

PRESIDENT'S WELCOME

Dear Readers:

The Society for the Study of Social Problems is pleased to offer you the *Agenda for Social Justice: Solutions 2012*. It represents an effort by our professional association to nourish a form of public sociology designed to be useful to policy makers. We also see it as a way of giving something back to the people who -- and institutions that -- participate in the challenging work of crafting progressive solutions to contemporary social problems.

Sincerely,

Wendy Simonds, Georgia State University
SSSP President, 2011-2012

EDITORIAL INTRODUCTION

The Society for the Study of Social Problems (SSSP) was formed in 1951 by social scientists interested in using social research to help in the solution of persistent social problems. This report – *Agenda for Social Justice: Solutions 2012* – is designed to broadly inform our readers about some of the nation's most pressing social problems and to propose policy responses to those problems. Our audience includes social science scholars, teachers, and students; social activists; journalists, policymakers; elected officials; and of course the public-at-large. In short, this book is our attempt to inform and contribute to the ongoing public discourse about the nature and amelioration of some of our society's social problems.

This release of this report is intended to coincide with the major U.S. elections taking place in 2012, and this *Agenda for Social Justice* is the third iteration of the effort (which has appeared in two earlier volumes: 2004 and 2008). The endeavor was inspired by Dr. Robert Perrucci in his 2000 SSSP Presidential Address, "Inventing Social Justice: SSSP and the 21st Century," in which he reminded the SSSP membership of the need to engage in public discourse with those who might use our academic and practical knowledge in addressing social problems.[i] Not only did Dr. Perrucci's speech mark the 50th Annual Meeting of the SSSP, it also helped set an agenda for our work moving into the 21st Century. From this inspiration a new committee was formed: the Justice 21 Committee, whose mission is to undertake the charge given by Dr. Perrucci to contribute to a public sociology of social problems.

In keeping with the spirit of the SSSP and the Justice 21 Committee, this report is disseminated at low cost and as widely as possible. This report is freely available electronically to the entire SSSP membership via the Society's website. In addition, the report is available at nominal costs in both electronic (Kindle) and print formats via the Amazon.com site, with proceeds supporting the missions of the SSSP and Justice 21 Committee. This report has also been disseminated free of charge to agencies working in progressive policy, media, and social justice. Finally, we have learned in recent years that we have a global audience, many of whom cannot afford to purchase this book, even at a nominal cost. Understanding the urgent need for reliable social science information among students, scholars, activists, and policymakers in less developed countries, we also have created a request form via which those who experience economic hardship may request a copy of our book free of charge.

However, it is the content of the book which matters most, and it is our hope that our readers will be inspired and informed by the content. This year's *Agenda for Social Justice* contains eleven chapters, each contributed by outstanding scholars in their respective areas, and each chapter addresses a specific social problem facing the U.S. today. Each piece can certainly stand on its own, and will certainly be informative in itself. The reader may also notice that each chapter follows a definite format, and that the content is divided into three major sections: the first defining the social problem, the second providing evidence available to outline the state of affairs, and third offering concrete suggestions for the types of policies that would be effective in ameliorating these problems.

The chapters in this book cover a wide range of concrete issues facing our society today, including issues of immigration, health, inequality, appropriation of public funds, income security, racial diversity, and social welfare. These are certainly among the pressing issues and discussions that one encounters in the news media and other areas of social discourse. Indeed it is our hope that our readers will devour the chapters in this book, and that they will take these arguments to their academic work (whether teaching or scholarship) and the ideas into action in the world, ultimately creating a more just society.

With best wishes,
Glenn W. Muschert
Chair, SSSP Justice 21 Committee

ACKNOWLEDGEMENTS

So many people provided assistance on this project, and it is of course in large part due to their contributions that we were able to produce this volume. We offer our sincere thanks to the following folks:

Jinjie (JJ) Chen, for marketing planning and help with marketing and distribution conceptualization, planning, and execution.

Helen Armstrong, for graphics design advice, assistance, pro bono services, and materials.

Michele Koontz and Sharon Shumaker, for organization and moral support.

Lisa East for production support and for services as web mistress,

The Justice 21 Committee:

Glenn W. Muschert (Chair), Miami University

Kathleen Ferraro, Northern Arizona University

Brian V. Klocke, State University of New York, Plattsburgh

JoAnn Miller, Purdue University

Robert Perrucci, Purdue University

Jon Shefner, University of Tennessee

CHAPTER 1

NINETEEN MILLION AND COUNTING: UNIQUE ISSUES FACING AMERICA'S FOREIGN-BORN WOMEN IN THE HOME AND WORKPLACE

Elizabeth J. Clifford, Ph.D.
Towson University

Susan C. Pearce, Ph.D.
Eastern Carolina University

Reena Tandon, Ph.D.
University of Toronto

They say women are not strong. But I am working here…When I left my country, I told myself, "I have to go and work, and I will do it." And here I faced all kinds of things, but I am here.

(*Lucia*, Mexican domestic worker)

THE PROBLEM

More than half of our foreign-born population in the United States is female. There are now 19,971,801 foreign-born women and girls who reside in the United States (American Community Survey, 2010 3-year estimates). This population includes those who are documented, undocumented, and naturalized citizens, encompassing all races, religions, class backgrounds, and 148 nationalities. U.S. immigration policy has yet to catch up with the increased diversity of this population. In contrast to women of previous generations, the majority of immigrant women (54 percent) work outside the home, and many are the lead pioneers in a family's chain migration. As a result of the cultural lag between the assumptions embedded in immigration law and this changing profile, many of the problems faced by immigrant women are in need of policy solutions.

An immigrant woman's livelihood and life chances are profoundly shaped both by her gender and the fact that she is foreign-born. While this is the case regardless of the time in history, the immigrant woman's difficulties are compounded in the current troubled American political and economic climate. Combine a post-9/11 insecurity over foreign threats with the unsettling and continuing outcomes of the 2008-2009 financial meltdown, and the country's foreign-born are the most convenient scapegoats. While often those under greatest suspicion and criticism are males, much of the fallout from the scapegoating lands on the backs of immigrant women.

In both the home and the workplace—and the world of domestic labor, which straddles both--the issues faced by immigrant women overlap with and are distinct from those faced by both native-born women and immigrant men. By examining both the home and the workplace, we cover the two institutions where immigrant women spend the majority of their waking—and sleeping—hours. Each carries its own particular dynamics related to immigration policy and practice. In this chapter, we first examine issues related to immigrant women's home lives: family reunification immigration policies and intimate partner violence. While many immigrant women benefit from family-based immigration policies, we argue that certain provisions serve to prevent many women from being able to sponsor their family members. Intimate partner violence is not a problem unique to immigrant women. However, being foreign-born makes women who experience violence in the home particularly vulnerable. In terms of the workplace, we examine the problems faced by foreign-born women in domestic work, where many of their co-workers are both immigrants and women. We also consider the obstacles immigrant women entrepreneurs, who are a growing population, face. After exploring these problems we recommend principle-based policy solutions. Our discussion of these issues is informed by our first-hand research that included interviews with immigrant women across nationalities.

THE RESEARCH

Home
Family-based immigration

The majority of family members sponsored for immigration are women and girls. Of course, women are not just sponsored, but also sponsor relatives. Not all women are equal in accessing family-based immigration policies, however.

- **Status matters.** Women that are undocumented are not able to sponsor family members.
- **Family type matters.** While many of those sponsored are spouses, our policies privilege heterosexual, married couples. Those who wish to sponsor same-sex spouses or common-law partners are unable to do so.
- **Income matters.** Sponsoring relatives' earnings must be at least 125% of the federal poverty line (U.S. Code, Title 8, Subchapter B, Part 213a). Since women's incomes still tend to be lower than men's, this requirement disproportionately prevents women from sponsoring relatives.

Intimate Partner Violence

Immigrant women who find themselves in a violent partnership face particular vulnerabilities.

- If they call the police and an arrest occurs, the batterer can now be deported—and many women reportedly recoil from making this call.

• If these women decide to leave a marriage they may also lose their immigration status. Spouses of certain non-immigrant employment visa-holders, such as the H1B visa, for example, are not authorized to work in the United States. This limits the women's status and potential income independence that would allow them to leave such a relationship.

Work

Immigrants contribute to the American economy, in over 300 occupations. For this chapter, we focus on issues for immigrant women in domestic work and entrepreneurship. We chose these particular fields because we wanted to include one that is traditionally and currently closely associated with immigrant women (domestic work), as well as a field in which immigrant women are emerging, and have begun to make great strides (entrepreneurship). While some of the issues we raise are unique to entrepreneurs and domestic workers, others would be shared to some extent by immigrant women in other fields of work.

Domestic Work

As indicated by the organization Domestic Workers United, the majority of today's domestic laborers in many communities are foreign-born. This occupation signifies a source of livelihood and potential abuse for women.

- **Domestic work provides sustenance to women and families**: Women are able to create meaning from this work, use it to transition to American society, and support working families through the household and childcare they provide.
- **Domestic work can be an exploitative form of labor**: Our research interviews uncovered a range of vulnerabilities that this population faces. We heard repeated accounts of low wages, no benefits, employer abuse, exploitation, and even sexual violence, due to the unregulated and the behind-closed-doors nature of this work.
- **Exploitation is embedded in policy**: There are broad gaps in labor law to protect this sector; for example, domestic workers are currently excluded from provisions of the National Labor Relations Act. This exclusion makes immigrant women in this occupation particularly

4

vulnerable, and also makes it more difficult for them to organize or otherwise seek redress.

Entrepreneurship

Immigrant women are more likely to be business owners than are native-born women, and are catching up to immigrant men's entrepreneurship rates. As of 2008, 38% of all immigrant business owners were women. Women are making great strides in this area, including in fields once reserved for men. Nevertheless, these women continue to meet blockages, such as access to start-up capital and presumptions that they are not able to run large firms or compete in fields atypical for women.

RECOMMENDATIONS AND SOLUTIONS

Public policies devoted to immigration, family, and employment law could benefit from a more diverse and accurate portrait of today's immigrants. The particular situations of women's lives should be carefully considered in the following ways when scripting policy reform.

Family

- **Broaden family-based immigration policies to reflect diversity.** The law largely assumes that a "family" fits a certain mold: a nuclear, legally married, heterosexual configuration with a male breadwinner and dependent children. Family-based immigration policies would benefit from more elasticity to accommodate varied conceptions of family and kin, and in particular, we urge the United States to follow the lead of many other nations that now allow sponsorship of same-sex and common-law partners. Given the importance of extended family members in many cultures, broader inclusion of such kin would also benefit many immigrant women. In addition, as women are on average paid less than men, removing financial restrictions governing who is allowed to sponsor relatives would likely allow more women to be reunited with family members. Finally, the law could equalize sponsorship options across citizen and noncitizen categories. Currently, there are fewer categories that noncitizens can sponsor, and they usually face a longer wait for sponsorship.

- **Expand public education and compliance with immigration remedies for domestic violence survivors.** Although immigrant and women's rights advocates have successfully won immigration remedies for those in abusive relationships through the Violence Against Women Act of 1996 (re-authorized in 2005) and the 2007 U visa for victims of crime, surveys indicate that few women are aware of these options and some groups of women more likely than others to successfully utilize them. Language and cultural barriers arise in court situations, for example, and immigrant women in certain types of families and personal-life configurations tend to be favored. More broadly, current criminal-justice approaches to domestic violence must be reconsidered, given that an arrest for such a violation can lead directly to deportation, making it less likely for reporting to occur.

- **Shift the focus of immigration enforcement away from practices that separate families.** As federal authorities have ramped up workplace raids, detentions, and deportations, immigrant family stability has been undermined, and foreign-born women have suffered. In two-parent families, the detention or deportation of one parent can leave the remaining family members in dire straits, with one less breadwinner. The situation is even more precarious for single-parent families, about 83% of which are headed by women (U.S. Census). If they are detained or deported, children might be left with no adult guardian. If other relatives are not available, children may enter the foster care system. Recent restrictive state laws such as those in Alabama and Arizona make the prospects of detention and deportation more imminent. After the passage of the new Alabama law, a domestic violence victim was told by a court clerk that she would be turned over to Immigration and Customs Enforcement if she moved forward with her report.

Workplace

Just as these women are actively building families and raising the next generation, they are contributing to the American economy and community stability. Foreign-born women are now occupying all of the social rungs of the work force—from the lowest-paid to higher echelons of academia and business.

Like men, foreign-born women offer a net benefit to the country, including caring for children, cleaning buildings and houses, teaching, creating artwork, starting companies that create jobs, and much more. These benefits could be enhanced by the following measures:

- **Increase the numbers and types of visas that could attract talented skilled labor.** This might include special visas for entrepreneurs, *au pairs,* teachers (with clear ways to transfer credentials), medical professionals, technology specialists, artists, musicians, among others.

- **Scrutinize gender stereotypes that may exist in distributing visas and employment opportunities.** A growing number of international engineering graduates—a key labor-market need—for example, are women. Are companies equally recruiting men and women? The market is also not tapping into a talent pool that is already in the country: professional "trailing spouses" of the holders of certain employment visas.

- **Expand the opportunities for start-up capital for immigrant women.** "Set-asides," such as contracts made available for minority businesses, have demonstrated their potential for reducing inequalities, but set-asides for female owners exist only for selected industries. Start-up capital, in the form of loans or venture capital investments, needs to be equally available across industries—including service industries—and in adequate amounts. The assumption that women are only running small businesses is no longer accurate.

In the arena of domestic employment, greater regulation and accountability is needed, including labor protections for worker organizing and for publicizing abuse by employers.

- **Expand existing labor laws** like Fair Labor Standards Act and National Labor Relations Act and protections under the Occupational Safety and Health Act (OSHA) to include domestic workers and extend measures now available to workers in some states such as the Domestic Workers Bill of Rights in New York. For workers on domestic work visas, extend protection to domestic workers who bring forth complaints of abuse against employers.

- **Ensure effective implementation of existing policy/legislation** and support dissemination of information regarding rights and protection available to domestic workers.

- **Change the terms of the debate on immigrant employment.** There is a hidden risk in publicizing our findings of immigrant women's employment contributions: the backlash against immigrants suspected of "taking jobs" from the native-born could start to fold women into that stereotype. Economists routinely observe, however, that there is no measurable finite number of jobs that a society can sustain, making this subtractive argument difficult to demonstrate. On the other hand, immigration rights arguments that immigrants are needed economically because "they do the jobs that Americans don't want"—including domestic labor—could have the unintended consequence of soft-pedaling efforts to raise the wages and benefits of marginal jobs so that they are considered respectable work by any worker.

As we learned from our interviews, immigrant women—like men—are often underemployed; the household worker with a university degree is not likely to agree that she "wants" such a job any more than a well-educated American would. Therefore, we recommend the following:

- Police compliance with the federal minimum wage and more locally based "living wages" indexed to local costs of living.
- Expand the availability of employment visas to meet the demand. This would make a serious dent in the development of a shadow economy in which no immigrant woman that we interviewed wanted to participate.

Across Home and Workplace

- **Relax the securitization culture—and its underlying laws and practices.** More broadly, these women will not feel safe or welcomed until the current enforcement culture, which lawyers are terming "crimmigration," subsides. While immigration law is technically a civil law, the border between civil and criminal law has been blurred as immigrants fill local jails and detention centers. Local and state laws, like those recently passed in Arizona and Alabama, exacerbate these concerns. The "hunting" of undocumented immigrants—often snaring or impacting the documented as well—which dovetails with the public scapegoating of the foreign born, affects families and workplaces in profound ways. In the words of *Lucia,* whose quote opened this chapter, immigrant women face "all kinds of things."

As immigrant women are becoming independent and primary earners and sponsors, they are also susceptible to both exploitative work conditions and family violence. Immigrant status and unsupportive laws and policies add to their vulnerability. As we are advocating for greater empowerment of women through policy reforms, we recommend at the same time, protective measures for them. Effective policies must take into account the interconnected nature of immigrant domains of home and work for women in particular.

In sum, immigration policy has to be more sensitive to gender issues, and other policies that impact the lives of immigrant women—from intimate partner violence laws to Small Business Administration loan guidelines—need to be more sensitive to immigration issues, in order for the more than 19 million foreign-born women and girls in our midst to be able to live full, rich lives in the United States.

KEY RESOURCES

"Background on Laws Affecting Battered Immigrant Women." 2011. Futures without Violence. Retrieved July 9, 2011 (http://www.futureswithoutviolence.org/userfiles/file/Immigrant Women/Background%20on%20Laws%20Affecting%20Battered% 20Immigrant%20Women.pdf).

Domestic Workers United and Datacenter. 2006. "Home Is Where The Work Is. Inside New York's Domestic Work Industry." Retrieved June 7, 2009 (www.domesticworkersunited.org/media.php?show=9).

Ely, Gretchen. 2004. "Domestic Violence and Immigrant Communities in the United States: A Review of Women's Unique Needs and Recommendations for Social Work Practice and Research." *Stress, Trauma, and Crisis: An International Journal* 7:223-41.

Hondagneu-Sotelo, Pierrette. ed. 2003. *Gender and U.S. Immigration: Contemporary Trends.* Berkeley and Los Angeles: Unive. of California.

Parreñas, Rhacel Salazar. 2001. *Servants of Globalization: Women, Migration, and Domestic Work.* Stanford, CA: Stanford University Press.

Pearce, Susan C., Elizabeth J. Clifford, and Reena Tandon. 2011. *Immigration and Women: Understanding the American Experience.* New York: NYU Press.

Philippa, Strum and Danielle Tarantolo, eds. 2003. *Women Immigrants in the United States.* Washington, DC: Woodrow Wilson International Center for Scholars.

Sokoloff, Natalie and Christina Pratt, eds. 2005. *Domestic Violence at the Margins: Readings on Race, Class, Gender, and Culture.* Piscataway, NJ: Rutgers University Press.

U.S. Census, "Children's Living Arrangements and Characteristics: March 2002." Table 8 (www.census.gov/prod/2003pubs/p20-547).

ABOUT THE AUTHORS

The authors of this chapter co-authored the book, *Immigration and Women: Understanding the American Experience,* New York University Press, 2011.

Elizabeth J. Clifford, Ph.D., is an Associate Professor of Sociology at Towson University, where she is also the Director of American Studies and Coordinator of the Baltimore Immigration Summit. In addition to research on immigrant women, she also is active in studying immigration in Baltimore, the portrayal of immigrants in young adult fiction, and historical discussions of immigration in the African American press.

Susan C. Pearce, Ph.D., is Assistant Professor of Sociology at East Carolina University. She conducts interview research on the issues that face immigrant women, with a focus on entrepreneurship, intimate partner violence, and activism, and has authored three special reports about immigrant women for the Immigration Policy Center. She has been engaged with immigrant-rights activism in the Baltimore-Washington DC corridor and Eastern North Carolina. Her research at the international level includes a focus on Eastern Europe and its transition to democracy.

Reena Tandon, Ph.D., teaches at the Centre for South Asian Studies, University of Toronto and is developing curricular service learning for the Faculty of Arts, Ryerson University. Her areas of interest include gender, labor, marginalization and civic engagement in transnational contexts. Current research projects include examining notions of rights and organizing of immigrant women workers. A community-engaged scholar, teacher and researcher, she affiliates closely with community-based organizations and groups in India, Canada and the United States.

CHAPTER 2

LEGISLATION IN THE PUBLIC INTEREST: REGULATORY CAPTURE AND CAMPAIGN REFORM

Amitai Etzioni, Ph.D.

George Washington University

THE PROBLEM

Liberals tend to favor regulations as expressions of the public will and the common good, and as a way to protect children, patients, mortgage holders, airline passengers, and many other consumers from abuse by unscrupulous actors in the private sector. Laissez-faire conservatives and libertarians tend to oppose regulations because they view them as an abusive use of the government's power and as harmful to the economic well-being of the nation.

I write "tend" because liberals recognize that some regulations are poorly crafted or not needed, and some conservatives and libertarians admit that some regulations are beneficial. However, each side demands that the other demonstrate why a deviation from their preferred default position is merited—and they set a fairly high bar that the introduction of regulations (or their removal) must first clear.

In addition, this is a case of pluralistic ignorance, in which various observers note incidents that deviate from their core assumptions, but neither generalize nor draw overarching conclusions from these incidents. Thus, liberals are quite aware of regulations that end up serving private interests rather than the public, but they still strongly favor regulations. For instance, they considered the enactment of the Dodd-Frank financial reform bill in 2010 to be one of the major achievements of the Obama administration, despite the fact that the bill had already been greatly diluted by lobbyists working for the industries it is supposed to regulate, and despite the fact that the law, as enacted by Congress, is particularly open-ended - leaving it to various agencies to shape the needed specifications, under conditions particularly favorable to lobbyists. Conservatives too may note incidents in which regulations serve those usually allied with them in the private sector, but nevertheless continue to be strongly opposed to regulation in general.

Both sides share one key assumption: they view regulations as acts of the government, largely aimed at the private sector, although they recognize that regulations do not always work in this way. In fact, the ways regulations are formulated and enforced are often deeply affected by the private sector. Economists and political scientists refer to this phenomenon as "regulatory capture." They show that regulations are often captured by those they are supposed to regulate, making the regulators and the regulated march more or less in tandem. Thierer and other scholars have found that regulatory capture has occurred "in various arenas: transportation and telecommunications; energy and environmental policy; farming and financial services; and many others." Nobel Laureate economist George Stigler, who is credited with having made major contributions to the study of capture, concludes that "as a rule, regulation is acquired by the industry and is designed and operated primarily for its benefit." I refer from here on to those who capture regulations as "special interests" in order to denote that these are often not groups which represent major segments of the electorate.

THE RESEARCH EVIDENCE

Some of those who have written about capture imply that it governs most, if not all, regulations and that capture is complete. Some have concluded from this observation that regulation is generally ineffective. In fact, however, there are considerable differences among different regulatory areas in the extent to which capture occurs. And although the level of capture is often significant, it is still far from complete. There follows here a brief illustration: a case study of a substantial—but not complete—capture of important regulations.

In 2001, Enron Corporation and its accounting firm Arthur Andersen were found to have used irregular accounting practices to conceal a significant amount of Enron's debts and losses. As these practices came to light, Enron's stock plummeted from over $90.00 to less than $.50 per share, forcing the company to declare bankruptcy, causing substantial losses to many thousands of investors, and leaving thousands of Enron employees without their retirement savings accounts and other benefits. Enron was not alone; similar scandals involved major other American corporations such as Tyco and WorldCom.

In response to these abuses, Congress passed the Sarbanes-Oxley Act in 2002. At the time, the law was considered by *The Economist* magazine to be "the most sweeping reform of corporate governance in America since the Great Depression in the 1930s." The law left working out the details of the new regulations to the Securities and Exchange Commission (SEC), which was subjected to extensive lobbying by the accounting industry, which was able to weaken its regulatory impacts. The bill initially banned auditors from providing their clients with advice on tax shelters (a particularly lucrative practice) because of fears that auditors would be inclined to soften their reviews in order not to lose the tax businesses, as well as concerns noted by *The Economist* that "if auditors were allowed to design tax shelters, they would end up auditing their own work, a conflict of interest." However, lobbyists convinced the SEC to allow auditors to provide tax services (though they must now obtain permission from the audit committee of the company's board of directors). The accounting industry's lobbyists won another victory when they used the SEC rule-writing process to weaken an older compromise they had made in 2000. That compromise required auditors to categorize their work as either auditing or non-auditing, and disclose to regulators the specific amounts they were paid for each. During the rule-writing process for Sarbanes-Oxley, the accountants modified this compromise to expand the definition of "auditing" work to include some tasks as "audit-related" and hence minimize the amount of "non-auditing" work they appeared to be doing.

Sarbanes-Oxley was further weakened in 2006. Instead of requiring auditors to investigate any accounting issues that have a "more than remote" chance of damaging a company's finances, the rules were revised to only require auditors to investigate issues that have a "reasonable possibility" of doing so. (The various thinning out of regulations are reflected in the size of the regulatory text of the law—it was reduced from 180 pages to 65 pages.) And in 2009, small businesses were permanently exempted from two of the acts key provisions—one requiring executives to confirm the integrity of their firm's internal accounting procedures, and another requiring an outside audit of these procedures.

Nevertheless, the law has achieved some of its goals. As John C. Coates of Harvard Law School has concluded, Sarbanes-Oxley "created new incentives for firms to spend money on internal controls, above and beyond the increases in audit costs that would have occurred after the corporate scandals of the early 2000s." Furthermore, Coates found, "Sarbanes-Oxley promises a variety of long-term benefits. Investors will face a lower risk of losses from fraud and theft, and benefit from more reliable financial reporting, greater transparency, and accountability," even if the difficulty of calculating the law's costs and benefits means that judgments of it "must be tentative and qualitative." In short, regulatory capture –when special interest groups, part of the private realm, deeply affect public measures in ways that lead those measures to serve the purposes of private actors (i.e. profit-making)—can frequently be substantial, but capture is far from complete or all-encompassing. It is a major way in which the private and the public are intertwined without their separation being obliterated.

Aside from diluting regulations, capture is achieved in several other ways, briefly illustrated here.

a) Special interests compose the regulations. Lobbyists representing the pharmaceutical industry literally composed the text of the 2003 bill that governs drug benefits for Medicare recipients. This benefit was initially estimated to cost $400 billion over 10 years; more recent estimates range as high as $1.2 trillion. Also, as composed by the lobbyists, the law prohibits the government from negotiating the prices of these drugs.

b) Weaken enforcement. According to a 2006 report by Schlosser, "cutbacks in staff and budgets reduced the number of food-safety inspections conducted by the F.D.A. to about 3,400 a year from 35,000 in the 1970s," and "the number of inspectors at the Agriculture Department has declined to 7,500 from 9,000."

In the late 1980s and early 1990s, the U.S. Sentencing Commission drafted sentencing guidelines that aimed to severely punish corporate crimes. The Commission acted after it found that previous penalties for corporations convicted of major crimes were very light. For instance, Eli Lilly & Company, the pharmaceutical manufacturer, was fined a mere $25,000 after pleading guilty to the charge of failing to inform the government of a large number of deaths caused by its arthritis drug Oraflex, as is required by law. In November 1989, the commission published its draft guidelines, introducing large fines up to $364 million for crimes that had previously resulted in fines of just tens of thousands of dollars. The draft led to intense lobbying by major corporations and trade associations. As a result, the Commission reduced the suggested penalties by as much as 97 percent. The Commission also provided a list of extenuating circumstances that allowed offending corporations to reduce easily the remaining penalties to small amounts, if not to zero.

c) Gaming the regulators. Special interests affect the regulatory regime in their favor by switching regulations into a new jurisdiction (e.g., from state to federal) or by pitting the regulators against one another. Thus, reports the *Washington Post*, when mortgage lender Countrywide Financial felt "pressured" by the federal agencies charged with overseeing it, executives "simply switched regulators." As a national commercial bank, Countrywide had been under the jurisdiction of the Office of the Comptroller of the Currency. As early as 2005, Countrywide executives engaged in talks with the Office of Thrift Supervision (OTS), known to be a much more "flexible" regulator. Less than two years later, Countrywide redefined itself as a "thrift" instead of a "national commercial bank" and thus became regulated by the OTS. Over the next two years OTS proved to be a very lax regulator of Countrywide's mortgage lending as it also proved to be for IndyMac, Washington Mutual, and other major lenders. They also played a significant role in the financial crisis that followed.

d) <u>Setting prices and rates</u>. Regulators are often charged with limiting the profits gained by one industry or another; e.g. for limiting the rate increases of utilities. However, in several major cases, captured regulations had the opposite effect: they bolstered the profits of a specific industry by setting higher prices and rates than the market would provide. One widely-cited example is the government-created Civil Aeronautics Board, which set airline fares and limited the entry of new airlines into the travel market. After airlines were deregulated in 1978, fares typically fell by 20% or more.

e) <u>Close relationships between regulators and industry</u>. After the explosion at Upper Big Branch Mine in West Virginia in 2010 killed 29 people, it was reported that the federal agency responsible for mine oversight, the Mine Safety and Health Administration, was reluctant to close even those mines which repeatedly violated safety rules. Furthermore, the agency rarely imposed large fines and often failed to collect the fines it did impose.

After the explosion at BP's Deepwater Horizon well in 2010, and the resulting oil spill in the Gulf of Mexico, there was widespread consensus that the federal agency responsible for regulating the well, the Minerals Management Service (MMS), had failed in large part because it had been captured. In the *Wall Street Journal*, Gerald P. O'Driscoll, Jr. wrote, "By all accounts, MMS operated as a rubber stamp for BP. It is a striking example of regulatory capture: Agencies tasked with protecting the public interest come to identify with the regulated industry and protect its interests against that of the public. The result: Government fails to protect the public." The Interior Department's inspector general found that MMS officials responsible for overseeing drilling in the Gulf of Mexico were allowing oil and gas officials to fill out their own inspection forms, and some even considered themselves part of the industry they were tasked to regulate.

All this shows that as far as regulations are concerned, the public and the private realms are often and significantly intertwined, that they change in tandem, and that they are co-determined—although there are no studies that show with any measure of precision the extent to which regulations across the board are captured. It is, however, clear that in those considerable areas in which capture—whether full, substantial, or merely partial—occurs, we face the same force from both realms, and that captured regulations neither serve the liberal vision of promoting the common good nor confirm the conservative fear that the government will impose its will on the private sector. Rather, they are instances in which the prevailing powers of the private realm prevail in the public realm as well.

RECOMMENDATIONS AND SOLUTIONS

Regulatory capture cannot be tackled by itself because it is but the tip of the iceberg. Large segments of what Congress does is captured by private interests, including the introduction of hundreds of loopholes into the tax code, earmarks and their functional equivalents, subsidies, and so and on. To overcome this widespread, generic capture would require a major change in the distribution of power within the American political system. Such changes are very difficult to bring about and occur rarely.

In some nations, they have entailed revolutions. In the U. S., they are much more likely to be driven by a major social movement. The progressive movement at the onset of the 20th century, the Civil Rights Movement, and the movement to protect the environment are key examples. Such movements first of all change core values and then mobilize large numbers of citizens to support new norms and policies that reflect these values.

Unfortunately, it seems that it is easier (although still far from easy) to form social movements around substantive issues rather than around procedural ones. Reforming the ways elections are financed—the main way capture takes place—is considered a procedural matter. This seems to be a key reason attempts to mobilize a reform movement around this issue by Common Cause and others have failed. One can argue, though, that Occupy Wall Street movements (and some may argue even the Tea Party) reflect new popular discontent with the political system that may lead to reforms. That is, unless these movements will themselves be captured.

KEY RESOURCES

Applebaum, Binyamin and Ellen Nakashima. 2008. "Banking Regulator Played Advocate Over Enforcer." *Washington Post*, November 23. Retrieved July 17, 2012 (http://www.washingtonpost.com/wp-dyn/content/article/2008/11/22/AR2008112202213.html).

Coates, John C. 2007. "The Goals and Promise of the Sarbanes-Oxley Act." *Journal of Economic Perspectives*, 21(1): 91-116.

Etzioni, Amitai. 1988. *The Moral Dimension: Toward a New Economics*. New York: The Free Press.

O'Driscoll, Gerald P., Jr. 2010. "The Gulf Spill, The Financial Crisis, and Government Failure." *Wall Street Journal*, June 12. Retrieved July 17, 2012 (http://online.wsj.com/article/SB1000142405274870457530457529 6873167457684.html).

Schlosser, Eric. 2006. "Has Politics Contaminated the Food Supply?" *New York Times*, December 11. Retrieved July 17, 2012 (http://www.nytimes.com/2006/12/11/opinion/11schlosser.html?pagewanted=all).

Stigler, George J. 1971. "The theory of economic regulation." *Bell Journal of Economics and Management Science* 2 (1): 3-21.

The Economist. 2003. "Setting the Rules." *The Economist*, January 29. Retrieved July 17, 2012 (http://www.economist.com/node/1558898).

Thierer, Adam. 2010. "Regulatory Capture: What the Experts Have Found." The Technology Liberation Front, December 19. Retrieved July 17, 2012 (http://techliberation.com/2010/12/19/regulatory-capture-what-the-experts-have-found/).

Winkler, Rolfe. 2009. "The race to the regulatory bottom continues." *Reuters*, Option ARMageddon Blog, November 4. Retrieved July 17, 2012 (http://blogs.reuters.com/rolfe-winkler/2009/11/04/the-race-to-the-regulatory-bottom-continues/).

ABOUT THE AUTHOR

Amitai Etzioni is a University Professor at The George Washington University. He has taught at Columbia, Harvard, and Berkeley. He is the author of *The Active Society* and 20 other books. He served as a senior advisor in the Carter White House. Richard Posner named him one of the top 100 American intellectuals. For more, see the following web pages: http://icps.gwu.edu/staff/amitai-etzioni/ and http://blog.amitaietzioni.org/.

CHAPTER 3

GOVERNANCE AND INNER-CITY SOCIAL PROBLEMS

Robert Grantham, Ph.D.

Bridgewater State University

THE PROBLEM

Residents of America's inner-cities continue to struggle with serious social and economic problems. Many believe the shifted policy priorities of federal governance during the early 1980s have contributed to and exacerbated these problems. In brief, shifts in governance in the U.S. over the last three decades have moved toward policies that are overly dependent on market strategies, downplaying the benefits of mixed economies. Shifts in governance resulted in reduced spending to cities and tax-cuts for upper income families and corporations, accompanied by assaults against industry regulations that have led to poor working conditions and unsafe consumer products. Many social problems scholars believe that shifts in governance have intensified negative social conditions, particularly inner-city poverty, residential instability, and vulnerabilities associated with single-parent families.

The task for this chapter is to provide some evidence of the problematic efforts of governance in large inner-cities and specific outcomes of the newly-adopted emphasis. At the end, I discuss potential solutions that may help to improve life for urban dwellers in general and inner-city residents in particular. I argue that decisions of governance are not harmless, but bear some culpability for inner-city conditions. I also provide examples of governance that have benefitted inner-city residents and communities.

THE EVIDENCE

Social problems scholars have examined the effects of the new relationships between federal and state governments, especially in connection with urban funding needs. For example, researcher Bryan Jones noted that cities have often had to rely heavily on "speculative budgeting" processes, often leading to city deficits being hidden in the anticipated federally funded portions of their municipal budgets. Thus, strained budgets often meant that large cities could no longer expect that federal financial support would help them to fund services to address persistent socio-economic problems of inner-city areas, like unemployment, rodent control, garbage collection, crumbling schools, and high rates of school attrition. This new relatively laissez faire relationship between the federal government and large cities is referred to as "New Federalism," which accelerated after the mid-1970s. In the context of the new relationship between government and cities, researchers note the following changes:

- Loss of federal aid: Paul Peterson of the Brookings Institution shows that national aid to big cities (in 1990 dollars) dropped from $9.3 billion in 1977 to below $5 billion in 1990. Per capita figures fell from $244 to $109.

- Budgetary constraints: Researchers Drier, Mollenkopf and Swantstom argue in *Places Matter* that urban budgetary constraints were exacerbated by the fact that state governments did not live up to expectations that they would compensate cities for losses in federal aid. They point out that in 1980, national funds accounted for 22% of big city budgets; as early as 1989 this number had dropped to about 6%.

- Decline in housing subsidies: In *A Right to Housing*, Peter Drier illustrates how Federal housing funds to support low-income families, in 1983, represented only 27% of total federal housing subsidies and fell to 7% by the year 2000. By comparison, subsidies for homeowners, such as the mortgage interest tax deduction, represented 59% of federal subsidies for housing, and actually grew by 10% over the same time period.

- Allocation of funds and cities: Recently, we continue to see evidence of a shifted trend in the relationship between cities and higher levels of government. The United States Conference of Mayors (USCM) maintains that urban areas are often "short-changed" by their respective state governors regarding the allocation of federal funding sources. The UCSM noted the following in June 2009 press releases:
    o "the three most congested cities in the U.S.—Los Angeles, New York, and Chicago— suffer from 26.5% of the nation's congestion costs, but receive[d] only 6.3% of federal surface transportation funds allocated" by their states as part of the American Recovery and Reinvestment Act (ARRA) of 2009.
    o urban "area unemployment levels will exceed 10%" by 2010, and "85% of the job losses during the recession will occur in the nation's 363 urban areas". Yet in Ohio, for example,

"Cleveland and Cincinnati, combined, account for 40% of the
state of Ohio's economy," but received less than 5% of what
was allocated to their state" by the federal government.
"Similarly, Indianapolis generates 39% of Indiana's economic
activity, and receive[d] only 4% of available ARRA funds
[awarded] to the state".

In general, historical data from the Office of Management and Budget show
that federal funds earmarked for education, training, employment, and
social services represented about 25% of federal outlays to state and local
governments in 1975. By 2009, this figure was down to roughly 12%. Many
proponents of this shift in governance argued that such changes in
governance were necessary, as inflation had climbed to 13.8% in 1980, up
from less than 4% in 1972. At the same time, unemployment had risen to
almost 9% in 1982 up from less than 5% in 1972. Those in favor of the
New Federalism argued that due to high wages of union workers and
government regulations, the United States was losing its competitive edge
globally. Essentially, proponents of the new shift in direction held that
government involvement in the economy is inefficient, and instead
proposed market-based approaches, which became and remain influential in
shaping contemporary public policy.

SOCIAL PROBLEMS SCHOLARS AND GOVERNANCE

Social problems scholars critical of the New Federalism argue that the
misappropriation of public and private resources adversely influences the
life-chances of families and individuals in all areas, especially those living in
the inner-cities. Specifically, the following social problems, for example,
may be linked to a style of governance that relies on market strategies:

- federal deregulation has led to banks leaving inner-city areas, making it
  more difficult for residents to establish conventional bank accounts;

- inner-city public schools are being undermined by privatization models
  that threaten equal access options for low income residents;

- municipal funds are often used to promote various entertainment venues, such as sports stadiums, that often displace residents in order to accommodate the "visitor class";

- major commercial and political actors collude in ways that undermine mandates regarding the replacement of demolished affordable housing units; and,

- "get tough on crime" policies have led to disproportionate rates of incarceration for minority males, particularly for non-violent offenses.

In light of these social problems, researchers, like sociologist Robert Bursik, have turned their attention to the role decisions of governance play in exacerbating urban conditions such as the vulnerabilities of single-parent families, residential instability, and persistently high levels of poverty. Their focus on government culpability challenges widespread and traditional views that lay blame on individual behavior for the persistence of inner-city problems. For example, for years some argued that moral deficiencies of residents, such as poor parenting skills, acceptance of violence, promiscuous behavior, and an inability to delay gratification, were the cause of social problems in inner-city neighborhoods. However, well known urban scholars, such as Elijah Anderson, Ruth Peterson and Laurie Krivo demonstrate that it is not cultural deficiencies, but the lack of access to resources like decent schools, home ownership, and stable jobs, which greatly increase crime rates and other problematic behavior among minority, inner-city males. In the context of a broader discussion about class, Paul Kingston relates hedonistic behavior to the notion of having or exercising a moral compass, and he illustrates that upper income groups (or social elites) are just as hedonistic—or in some cases more so than—lower income groups.

Rather than focus on individual pathology, researchers ask whether "decisions of government" contribute to making single-parents, low-income families, and those concentrated in residentially unstable neighborhoods more vulnerable to social problems. The following examples illustrate research that identifies acts of governance that contribute directly to inner-city social problems relative to single parenthood, residential instability, and poverty.

Single Parent Families

- In a Hartford, Connecticut study, Himmelgreen et. al., found that food insecurity and hunger among children between one and six years of age in single parent homes is partly explained by families running out of monthly food assistance, a direct outcome of government decisions about funding food support.

- A study by Cook and Bruin shows that black single mothers in central cities who receive housing assistance are ten times more likely to live in deficient housing than are those in other racial groups, which raises questions about equitable standards regarding how affordable housing programs are administered.

- In a Worcester, Massachusetts study, researchers Weinreb, et. al., found that the mental health of low income single mothers worsened over a ten year period, showing increases in major depressive illnesses and post-traumatic stress disorders. This increase coincides with major cuts in state budgets for mental health services.

- Welfare-to-work programs have been a mixed bag for single mothers. Social scientists like Ellen Reese show how the Personal Responsibility and Work Opportunity Reconciliation Act passed by Congress in 1996 has forced mothers to accept low wage jobs that often do not cover the costs of medical care and child care. Additionally, failure to comply with work requirements results in severe sanctions, including exclusion from future benefits.

- Finally, Michael Tonry and many criminologists argue that the "war on drugs" of the 1980s disproportionately targeted inner-city minority males, leading to high rates of incarceration for non-violent offenses. Scholars Coontz and Folbre explain that imprisonment had a significant effect on black families by reducing the number of marriageable men, and the presence of black fathers in urban neighborhoods.

Residential Instability

- Construction of new sports arenas in cities like St. Louis, Houston, and Los Angeles ignore the needs of urban residents, particularly inner-city residents, in favor of new stadium projects that are often promoted by city officials because they are believed to spur positive economic development. However, these projects often involve significant displacements of long-term residents, while accommodating an influx of non-residents, whom Peter Eisinger refers to as the "visitor class".

- In one study, Jason Hackworth examined the relationship between financial intermediaries and government officials. He argues specifically that bond rating agencies have gained enormous influence over the viability of cities and found that organizations like Standard & Poor's, Moody's, and Fitch—in conjunction with complicit public officials and economic developers—played a significant role in undermining affordable housing policies in cities like Detroit, New York, and Philadelphia.

- While public schools are often considered the embodiment of stability and security or *the great equalizer*, scholars note political efforts that help transform public schools into a competition for access between high and low income families, affecting even those residents who reside in the same neighborhoods. For example, Mary Patillo explains how a neighborhood in Chicago was gentrified through school reforms with traits of privatization that included "selective enrollment criteria" favoring incoming middle-class black families at the expense of lower-income black families who were often the original residents of the area.

Low Income/Poverty

Residents of low-income neighborhoods must struggle with conditions unique to their areas that have been exacerbated by government policies.

- Researchers Squires and O'Connor note that regulations in the banking industry facilitated the emergence of a two-tiered banking system, where high-interest check cashing businesses moved into inner-city areas in Milwaukee and elsewhere, as local banks slowly moved from central cities.

- Chung and Meyers found that inner-city residents in Minneapolis, despite lower incomes, consistently pay more for groceries than suburban residents. Some researchers have even referred to higher prices of groceries and goods and services that inner-city residents pay as a "ghetto tax" or "poverty tax".

- A study conducted by Joassart-Marcelli and Musso discovered that the allocation of federal funds to cities in Southern California was lower for cities with higher levels of poverty and as well as higher proportions of racial and ethnic minorities and immigrants. Thus, the distribution of federal expenditures increased rather than ameliorated income disparities across cities and exacerbated racial and ethnic differences in wealth.

The evidence I have discussed above illustrates the role governance plays in shaping the lives of vulnerable inner-city residents. Below, however, I discuss potential solutions that the general public and policy analysts might consider relative to the role and expectations of governance.

TOWARD POTENTIAL SOLUTIONS

Toward Job Creation

In response to the unique situation of troubled inner-city areas in the U.S., empowerment zones (EZs) were developed in the early 90s. The EZs were designed to provide handsome tax incentives for businesses that invested in inner-city areas, hopefully leading to the revitalization of the areas by creating jobs and increasing property values. This is a step in the right direction, as single parents, low-income families and the stability of residential areas can only stand to gain from an enhanced opportunity structure. Some of these programs have been successful, yet policy analysts and legislators need to be more vigilant in their efforts to build and improve upon the elements of successful programs.

- Jennings examined the influence of EZs in Boston, Massachusetts between 1999 and 2009 and concluded that they "helped to revitalize some of the poorest neighborhood areas (p. 63)," with the creation of local black-owned businesses and expansion of community organizations serving distressed parts of Boston that had been previously overlooked. The study also gives evidence that community involvement is an essential part of the effectiveness of EZs in inner-city areas.

- Rich and Stoker suggest that important city characteristics, such as strong local governance structures help to explain the success of some local EZs over others. On the national level, quantitative research by Wallace showed a level of political favoritism in which cities received federal support for EZs. Political favoritism, which can limit the effectiveness of EZ programs nationally, should be eliminated in the implementation of EZs.

- Researchers also suggest that in order for EZs to be the most effective, job training and education must be an important part of implementation. In other words, residents should be assisted in acquiring the skills and education required to obtain jobs created through EZs.

Toward Housing/Residential Stability

Recent reports about rising foreclosure rates in inner-cities are very troublesome for both renters and homeowners. However, the "burden of rent" as a major determinant of inner city residential problems, makes the suggestions listed below especially important.

- Availability of housing. As energy prices, foreclosures, and entertainment venues are pushing more suburbanites to seek residency closer to cities, inner-city residents are being displaced. Legislators may need to develop federal and or state standards that prohibit zoning ordinances in suburban areas that strictly limit the construction of multiple-family housing units.

- Affordability of housing. Analysts from *The Economist* and *Time* magazine suggest that we should reconsider our governmental commitment to homeownership. Policy analysts argue that homeownership in the U.S. has been over-promoted to the detriment of inner cities and low income areas. They argue instead that supports for renting may have a more positive effect on the affordability of housing. Additionally, they suggest eliminating or decreasing the deductions that homeowners are allowed to take for mortgage-interest payments, which in 2009 represented $80 billion in lost revenues. Essentially, many social scientists believe that higher percentages of renters in a given area are not necessarily problematic. For example, in Switzerland the majority of families rent their homes.

- Property foreclosures. Many inner-city residents have been displaced by property foreclosures. Some cities have instituted policies that require a two month notice before eviction. Others have purchased foreclosed properties and converted them to affordable apartments. This option prevents evictions and creates more low-income housing for inner-city renters.

Toward Socio-Economic Stability

Inner-city residents have experienced more dramatic increases in poverty during the recent recession than other group. For example, city-level poverty rose, according to the Urban Institute, from 16.5 to 17.7% (2007-2008) compared to surrounding suburbs where poverty rates rose from 9 to 9.8%. Media depictions of social problems tend to focus on the deviance of low-income inner-city dwellers, especially black and Latino men and contribute to negative public perceptions of these groups. There is current evidence of programs that have enjoyed some success in helping to alleviate rising poverty and controlling negative imagery of inner-city residents. Listed below are two examples of the types of anti-poverty programs that have been empirically tested and one example of a policy suggestion designed to inspire "anti-demonization" policies aimed at controlling discriminatory media representations.

- The Earned Income Tax Credit (EITC) is a mechanism designed to address poverty in the U.S. The Internal Revenue Service (IRS) describes the program as a credit for eligible people who work and have low wages. It reduces the amount of taxes owed and may even provide refunds for some individuals and families. Research has demonstrated the positive impact of EITC on low-income households, significantly lowering the poverty rate. The EITC has the largest impact on single parent households, lowering their poverty gap by almost one-third.

- Living Wage Initiatives. Many believe that current minimum wage requirements do not help families cope with the high costs of living. Instead, the idea of a living wage has been the topic of much discussion. A living wage is locally specific and considers the costs of basic expenses faced by families. Research on the effects of living wage laws in large cities indicates that they reduce urban poverty without increasing the depth of poverty among families that remain poor.

- Dealing with Negative Imagery. Many believe that TV programming, news broadcasts, and newspapers help to make caricatures or "folk devils" out of inner-city minority groups, particularly black and Hispanic males. This distorted imagery in the media has negative social consequences, including implicit biases against minority groups that affect hiring practices. A UCLA law professor Jerry Kang links excessive coverage of crime in the media to "implicit bias" that exists in society against minority groups, which also influences practices of bias in job hiring. One recommendation Kang makes—because of the role the media help to play in demonizing minority groups—is that FCC rules should be adopted that prohibits local news stations from excessive coverage of crime stories.

CONCLUSION

The shifts in governance that accelerated after the 1970s have diminished the resources devoted to ameliorating inner-city social problems. This shift was justified, in part, by focusing blame on inner-city residents for individual deficiencies and over-reliance on market-based solutions to problems of single parenthood, residential instability, and poverty. There are examples, however, of innovative strategies of governance that help to solve these problems. I have offered these examples as evidence that inner-city social problems are responsive to effective governance.

KEY RESOURCES

Acs, Gregory. 2009. "Poverty in the United States 2008." *The Urban Institute*, September 10. Retrieved July 24 (http://www.urban.org/publications/901284.html).

Adams, Scott and David Neumark. 2005. "Living Wage Effects: New and Improved Evidence." *Economic Development Quarterly* 19(1): 80-102.

Anderson, Elijah. 1999. *Code of the Streets: Decency, Violence, and the Moral Life of the Inner City*. New York: Norton.

Bursik, Robert J. 1989. "Political Decision-making and Ecological Models of Delinquency; Conflict and Consensus." Pp. 105-118 in *Theoretical Integration in the Study of Deviance and Crime: Problems and Prospects*, edited by S. F. Messner, M. D. Krohn, and A. E. Liska. Albany, NY: State University of New York Press.

Chung, Chanjin and Myers, Samuel L., Jr. 1999. "Do the Poor Pay More for Food? an Analysis of Grocery Store Availability and Food Price Disparities." *The Journal of Consumer Affairs* 33(2):276-296.

Cook, Christine C. and Marilyn J. Bruin. 1994. "Determinants of Housing Quality: A Comparison of White, African-American, and Hispanic Single-Parent Women." *Journal of Family and Economic Issues* 15(4): 329-347.

Coontz, Stephanie and Nancy Folbre. 2010 "Briefing Paper: Marriage, Poverty, and Public Policy." Pp. 185-196 in *Families as They Really Are*, Edited by Barbara J. Risman. New York: Norton Books.

Dreier, Peter. 2006. "Federal Housing Subsidies: Who Benefits and Why?: Pp. 105-138 in *A Right to Housing: Foundation for a New Social Agenda*, edited by R. G. Bratt, M. E. Stone, and C. Hartman. Temple, PA: Temple University Press.

Dreier, Peter, John H. Mollenkopf and Todd Swanstrom. 2001. *Place Matters: Metropolitics for the Twenty-first Century*. Lawrence, Kansas:

University Press of Kansas.

Economist. 2009. "Shelter, or Burden?" *The Economist,* April 16. Retrieved July 24 (http://www.economist.com/node/13491933).

Eisinger, Peter. 2000. "The Politics of Bread and Circuses: Building the City for the Visitor Class." *Urban Affairs Review* 35(3): 316-333.

Fraser, James C. and Edward L. Kick. 2007. "The Role of Public, Private, Non-Profit and Community Sectors in Shaping Mixed-Income Housing Outcomes in the US." *Urban Studies* 44(12): 2357-2377.

Hackworth, Jason. 2000. *The Neoliberal City: Governance, Ideology and Development in American Urbanism,* Ithaca, NY: Cornell University Press.

Himmelgreen, David A., Rafael Perez-Escamilla, Sofia Segura-Millan, Yu-Kuei Peng, Anir Gonzalez, Merrill Singer and Ann Ferris. 2000. "Food Insecurity among Low-Income Hispanics in Hartford, Connecticut: Implications for Public Health Policy." *Human Organization* 59(3): 334-342.

Huffington, Arianna. 2003. *Pigs at the Trough: How Corporate Greed and Political Corruption Are Undermining America.* New York: Crown Publishers.

Jennings, James. 2011. "The Empowerment Zone in Boston, Massachusetts 2000-2009: Lessons Learned for Neighborhood Revitalization." *Review of Black Political Economy* 38(1): 63-81.

Joassart-Marcelli, Pascale and Juliet A. Musso. 2001. "The Distributive Impact of Federal Fiscal Policy, Federal Spending and Southern California Cities." *Urban Affairs Review* 37(2): 163-183.

Jones, Byran D. 1986. "Speculative City Budgeting and Federal Grants." *Research in Urban Policy* 2:3-21.

Kang, Jerry. 2005. "Trojan Horses of Race" *Harvard Law Review* 118(5): 1489- 1593.

Kingston, Paul. 2000. *The Classless Society.* Stanford, CA: Stanford University Press.

Kiviat, Barbara. 2010. "The Case Against Home Ownership." *Time* magazine, September 11. Retrieved July 24 (http://www.time.com/time/magazine/article/0,9171,2013850,00. html).

Lipsitz, George. 1984. "Sports Stadia and Urban Development: A Tale of Three Cities." *Journal of Sport and Social Issues* 8(2): 1-18.

OMB. 2012. "Historical Tables - Budget of the U.S. Government FY 2013." *Office of Management and Budget.* Washington, DC: U.S. Government Printing Office. Retrieved July 24 (http://www.whitehouse.gov/sites/default/files/omb/budget/fy2 013/assets/hist.pdf).

Pattillo, Mary. 2007. *Black on the Block: The Politics of Race and Class in the City.* Chicago, IL: University of Chicago Press.

Peterson, Paul E. 1995. *The Price of Federalism.* Washington D.C.: Brookings Institution.

Peterson, Ruth D. and Lauren J. Krivo. 2005. "Macrostructural Analyses of Race, Ethnicity, and Violent Crime: Recent Lessons and New Directions for Research." *Annual Review of Sociology* 31(1): 331-356.

Reese, Ellen. 2007. "The Causes and Consequences U.S. Welfare Retrenchment." *Journal of Poverty* 11(3): 47-63.

Rich, Michael J. and Robert P. Stoker. 2010. "Rethinking Empowerment: Evidence from Local Empowerment Zone Programs." *Urban Affairs Review* 45(6): 775-796.

Squires, Gregory D. and Sally O'Connor. 1998. "Fringe Banking in Milwaukee: The Rise of Check-Cashing Businesses and the Emergence of a Two-Tiered Banking System." *Urban Affairs Review* 34(1): 126-149.

Tonry, Michael. 1995. *Malign Neglect: Race, Crime, and Punishment in America.* New York: Oxford University Press.

USCM. 2009. "The Nation's Mayors Commend Oberstar's Plan for Metropolitan Mobility." *The United States Conference of Mayors,* June 18, press release. Retrieved July 24 http://www.usmayors.org/pressreleases/uploads/RELEASENICK ELSOBERSTARTRANSBLUEPRINT609.pdf.

USCM. 2009. "Economic Study Shows U.S. Metropolitan Areas

Shortchanged in Stimulus Infrastructure Spending." *The United States Conference of Mayors*, June 12, press release. Retrieved July 24 http://usmayors.org/pressreleases/uploads/release-20090612-trans.pdf.

Wallace, Marc. A. 2004. "Congressional Considerations and Urban Characteristics in the Selection of Empowerment Zones and Enterprise Communities" *Journal of Urban Affairs* 26(5): 593-609.

Weinreb, Linda F., John C Buckner, Valerie Williams and Joanne Nicholson. 2006. "A Comparison of the Health and Mental Health Status of Homeless Mothers in Worcester, Mass: 1993 and 2003." *American Journal of Public Health* 96(8): 1444-1448.

ABOUT THE AUTHOR

Robert Grantham, Ph.D. is an Assistant Professor in the Department of Criminal Justice at Bridgewater State University in Massachusetts. His research interests are in urban crime, federal and state governance, and urban sociology. He is co-editor of *Urban Society: A Shame of Governance* recently published in 2010. His current research activities include examining aspects of policy in relationship to ongoing urban social problems, like social disorganization, crime, and the theoretical implications of the evidence of any links between policy and poor urban conditions.

CHAPTER 4

CRITICAL DIVERSITY IN AMERICA: DIVIDED PUBLIC OPINION AND CRITICAL POLICY DIRECTIONS

Cedric Herring, Ph.D.
University of Illinois at Chicago

THE PROBLEM

As the demography of the nation continues to change, diversity has become a critically important topic that poses philosophical, political and policy challenges. For many people, diversity is a good thing because it helps remove barriers that have historically prevented access to people of color, women, members of the lesbian, gay, bisexual, and transgender (LGBT) community, the disabled, and others who have been under-represented in the corridors of power. Increasingly, however, skeptics of diversity have become more cynical about the benefits of diversity. They claim that it divides America into separate groups by race, ethnicity, gender, etc. In so doing, they argue, diversity suggests that some social categories are more deserving of privileges than are others. There is also the argument that greater diversity is associated with lower quality because it places lower performing people in positions for which they are not suited. In short, skeptics of diversity suggest that group differences result in conflict and several costs. How should Americans live together? How should the state respond when the preferences and interests of groups are in conflict with each other? What should America's approach to diversity be?

Government can respond to diversity in a variety of ways. It can use a range of policy instruments such as prevention, discouragement, encouragement, and enforcement. Concrete policy issues that touch on debates about diversity include controversial topics such as affirmative action, gay marriage, immigration policy, and other contentious policy issues. Ultimately, policymakers need to be sensitive about the issues at stake and informed about the implications of their choices. This essay provides a brief discussion of the changing meanings of diversity, a summary of public opinion concerning policy issues that relate to diversity, and some critical policy recommendations.

For some people, the term "diversity" provokes intense emotional reactions because it brings to mind such politically charged ideas as "quotas;" yet, at its base the term merely refers to human qualities that make people different from one another. Dimensions of diversity include but are not limited to race, ethnicity, gender, sexual orientation, religion, age, physical abilities, geographic location, and class and socioeconomic status. More useful, however is the concept "critical diversity." As defined in Cedric Herring and Loren Henderson's (forthcoming) book Critical Diversity: The New Case for Inclusion and Equal Opportunity, critical diversity can be defined as the equal inclusion of people from varied backgrounds on a parity basis throughout all ranks of an organization. It especially refers to inclusion of those who are considered to be different from traditional members because of exclusionary practices. It also refers to inclusive organizational cultures that value and use the talents of all would-be members and includes them throughout all ranks of the organization. Critical diversity is an all-inclusive term, but battle lines are often drawn around which different groups are to be included and which groups can legitimately be discriminated against. In essence, discussions about critical diversity should not only contain observance and celebration of difference, but also examination of concepts such as equity, parity, fairness, inclusion of the previously excluded, etc.

THE RESEARCH EVIDENCE

Americans are split over many of the policy proposals that revolve around issues of diversity and inclusion. Illustrative of this are current debates surrounding such policy issues as affirmative action, immigration, and gay rights. To the degree that demographic subpopulations differ in their priorities and policy preferences, shifts in America's population base are likely to have an impact on public opinion on several policy issues and priorities. It is, therefore, informative to understand public opinion about various diversity and inclusion policy options.

Americans are deeply divided by race on the issue of affirmative action. There is also a gap by gender. In particular, according to a 2010 NBC/Wall Street Journal poll, 81% of African Americans support the view that "affirmative action programs are still needed to counteract the effects of discrimination against minorities, and are a good idea as long as there are no rigid quotas." More than two-thirds of Hispanic respondents (69%) support this view. But only 39% of whites are supportive of such policies. Women (56%) are also more likely than are men (49%) to support affirmative action to redress past discrimination.

Americans also disagree about the issue of immigration. In particular, a 2011 Pew Research Center poll, asked respondents "What should be the priority for dealing with illegal immigration in the U.S.?" Nearly 8 in 10 (79%) of non-Hispanic whites said that the focus should be on better border security and stronger enforcement of our immigration laws. More than three-quarters (76%) of Hispanic respondents said they believe the focus should be on creating a way for illegal immigrants already here to become citizens. Similarly, 70% of non-Hispanic whites approved of an Arizona law that requires police to verify the legal status of someone they have already stopped or arrested if they suspect that the person is in the country illegally. Two-thirds (66%) of Hispanics disapprove of the Arizona law.

A final kind of diversity and inclusion policy issue involves gay rights. In this instance, the issue is whether members of the LGBT community should be denied the right to marry. Nearly two-thirds (63%) of those with ties to the LGBT community oppose a constitutional amendment banning gay marriage. Still, according to data from a 2011 USA Today/ Gallup poll, nearly half (48%) of the general population believes that marriages between same-sex couples should not be recognized as being valid.

Despite the rather deep socio-demographic and political divides surrounding public policy issues related to diversity, there is ample evidence that diversity provides tangible benefits. Using data from a nationally representative sample of business organizations, Cedric Herring (2009) in an article in the American Sociological Review, showed that diversity is associated with increased sales revenue, more customers, greater market share, and greater relative profits. These results were consistent with arguments that a diverse workforce is good for business and that diversity offers a direct return on investment that promises greater corporate profits and earnings. A 2004 article in the Journal of Social Issues found that diversity provides creative conflict that leads to closer examination of assumptions so that people from varied backgrounds can create complex learning environments that lead to better solutions to problems. And, in its 2003 Amicus brief to the U.S. Supreme Court, the American Sociological Association put forth "an extensive body of scholarship demonstrating that race and ethnicity profoundly affect both the life experiences of individuals and the way individuals are treated within society."

CRITICAL DIVERSITY POLICY RECOMMENDATIONS AND SOLUTIONS

Go beyond just celebrating diversity and make sure to include people on an equitable basis.

Target and redistribute goods and resources to people who originate from traditionally excluded, disenfranchised, or other "disprivileged" groups that have historically been the victims of discrimination. Doing so will allow for an expansive notion of diversity, and it will call attention to distributive justice and its link to diversity. This will mean reconnecting diversity to affirmative action and the need to offset historical and ongoing racial and gender discrimination, segregation, and bias. In other words, it is necessary to reconnect diversity to compensatory justice—the idea that people should be fairly compensated for their injuries by those who have injured them. Americans should be reminded that affirmative action was instituted to improve the educational and employment opportunities for groups that historically had suffered discrimination in the educational sector and in the labor market.

Provide better access to education to the "disprivileged."
Institutions can proactively consider applicants' socioeconomic status, not only as part of consideration for financial assistance, but also as part of the admissions process itself. Based on the premise that those who start at the bottom have farther to go in order to make it to the top, educational institutions should select those from disprivileged backgrounds when choosing among equally or near equally qualified applicants according to conventional indicators. Similarly, they should select first-generation applicants rather than "legacies" or the offspring of alumni. In addition, colleges should include in their admissions criteria special consideration for applicants who have endured residential instability (e.g., homelessness, migratory work patterns, etc.) or other residential hardships. Along the same lines, universities should view high-achieving students who come from low-performing schools in a positive light. Too often, universities do the opposite and instead view mediocre students from elite (prep) schools as being meritorious.

Institutions can also implement plans that guarantee admission to a top percentile of students graduating from all in-state high schools or even subsets of schools. In many cases, such plans take advantage of the unfortunate existence of residential segregation to provide more racial diversity. Such plans also indirectly lead to more diversity at the high school level. They also allow some students of color who have not been admitted historically the opportunity to demonstrate their merit.

Provide pro-active policies in the workplace.

Tangible recruitment and retention strategies that companies employ (or avoid) can make a difference. Offering job training opportunities for employees of color and encouraging them to keep their skills current so that they can advance appears to pay dividends in correcting inequalities. Establishments that offer formal job training are more diverse than those that do not offer such opportunities, and those that proactively select people of color for job training rather than let employees self-select are also more diverse. And those establishments that reward people of color to keep their skills current have the opportunity to do even better, as employers that encourage employees to keep their skills current are more diverse than those that do not pursue such efforts. Also, establishments can take advantage of transparency. The results show that establishments that do things as simple as posting information about job vacancies and use internal hiring strategies (and presumably promote from within) are more diverse. Again, establishments can use such strategies, especially with employees of color to enhance their diversity. These results are consistent with the idea that organizations that foster climates that are inviting to racial and ethnic minorities and actively seek to promote them have more success in retaining them.

Many of these recruitment and retention efforts go hand-in-hand with signaling the importance of fairness in employment practices and the provision of job benefits that make it easier for establishments to be inclusive. Several due process issues and working conditions matter to a company's racial/ethnic diversity: The presence of an affirmative action department, job security, written job descriptions, formal performance evaluation processes, group incentives, job rotation, and incentives to learn new skills. More, the availability of daycare facilities or subsidies appear to pay dividends in terms of achieving racial and gender diversity.

Resist attempts to reverse diversity policies.

Diversity has been a governmental issue since people of color, women, members of the LGBT community, and other previously excluded or disadvantaged groups have pressed the government for greater inclusion. For many years, governmental initiatives were all that were in place to direct corporate diversity and to give excluded groups opportunities to succeed. It has only been within the last few decades that more and more companies have begun to realize that, as the country continues to become more diverse, their success will be tied to issues of diversity and inclusion. This becomes even more apparent when reviewing population trends that are moving towards a more diverse total population and a shrinking straight white male population that is native to this country.

It is important to demonstrate to organizational members that diversity is institutionally beneficial. In the business world, diversity produces positive outcomes over homogeneity because growth and innovation may depend on people from various backgrounds working together and capitalizing on their differences, as indicated in the author's 2009 article in the American Sociological Review. Although such differences may lead to some communication barriers and group conflict, diversity increases the opportunity for creativity and the quality of the product of group work. Diversity provides a competitive advantage through social complexity at the firm level when it is positioned within the proper context. In addition, linking diversity to the idea of parity makes it easier to see that diversity pays because organizations that draw on more inclusive talent pools are more successful. Diversity is positively related to organizational success because it allows organizations to "think outside the box" by bringing previously excluded groups inside the box, and thereby, enhancing creativity, problem solving, and performance.

CONCLUSIONS

So, to return to the initial set of questions: How should Americans live together? How should the state respond when the preferences and interests of groups are in conflict with each other? What should America's approach to diversity be? Policy leaders will need to foster cultural understanding, partnership and good will. They will need to fight the temptation to exploit cultural differences for short-term political gain. They will need to encourage cross-cultural and inter-faith dialogue, seek common ground and build relationships based on trust and mutual respect. More generally, those in positions of power and responsibility will need to focus on shared humanity despite political and policy differences. They will need to be able to lead citizens to work through their differences and deal with the inevitable policy tensions in a constructive manner.

Nationwide, there are proposals that could curtail diversity efforts, as exemplified by the following. In 2011, Georgia, South Carolina, Alabama, Indiana, and Utah enacted harsh anti-immigrant legislation modeled after Arizona's law. But the key provisions of each of these laws—like the Arizona law that inspired them—have been blocked by federal judges. There are also proposals under consideration that would limit the use of affirmative action and, therefore, limit access to higher education for many racial minority students. In particular, proponents of the Michigan Civil Rights Initiative which banned the use of affirmative action in institutions of higher education in Michigan have identified two dozen other states as likely targets for similar initiatives.

As mentioned above, government can respond to diversity by encouraging it, discouraging it, by ignoring it, etc. Ultimately, policymakers need to be sensitive about the issues at stake and informed about the implications of their choices. Doing so will require honesty, good faith, and mutual respect. The process is important. It will call for openness, consultation, dialogue, and participation. Those working through such processes must be willing to confront the hard issues, and they will need to recognize distinctive historical and cultural experiences that have set the different paths for diverse groups. All sides need to be willing to find solutions to the hard issues that continue to divide the nation.

☐

KEY RESOURCES

American Sociological Association et al. 2003. *Brief of the American Sociological Association, et al., as* Amici Curiae *in Support of Respondents.* Washington, DC: American Sociological Association.

Gurin, Patricia, Biren (Ratnesh) A. Nagda, and Gretchen E. Lopez. 2004. "The Benefits of Diversity in Education for Democratic Citizenship." *Journal of Social Issues* 60:17-34.

Herring, Cedric. 2009. "Does Diversity Pay? Race, Gender and the Business Case for Diversity." *American Sociological Review* 74:208-224.

Herring, Cedric and Loren Henderson. Forthcoming. *Critical Diversity: The New Case for Inclusion and Equal Opportunity.* Chicago: Diverse Solutions.

ABOUT THE AUTHOR

Cedric Herring, Ph.D. is Professor of Sociology and Public Policy at the University of Illinois at Chicago and Director of the Race and Public Policy Program in the Institute of Government and Public Affairs at the University of Illinois. Dr. Herring is former national President of the Association of Black Sociologists. He has published 7 books and more than 60 scholarly articles. His forthcoming book is Critical Diversity: The New Case for Inclusion and Equal Opportunity. He has shared his findings in community forums, in newspapers and magazines, on radio and television, before government officials, and at the United Nations.

☐

CHAPTER 5

GREATEST RISK OF INFECTION: YOUNG BLACK WOMEN AND SEXUALLY TRANSMITTED INFECTIONS

Tamara G.J. Leech, Ph.D.
Indiana University, Purdue University, Indianapolis

Devon J. Hensel, Ph.D.
Indiana University School of Medicine

THE PROBLEM

In the United States, Black women have disproportionately high rates of several sexually transmitted infections (STIs), including chlamydia, syphilis, gonorrhea and HIV/AIDS. In 2009, chlamydia rates in this population were nearly eight times higher than the rate among White women, affecting one out of every ten young Black women aged 15 to 19 years. Rates of syphilis in Black women doubled between 2005 and 2009, with resulting acquisition rates 29 times higher than among White women. Furthermore, at some point in her lifetime, one in 32 Black women will contract HIV (representing an acquisition rate three times that experienced by Hispanic/Latina women, and 15 times the rate among White women).

These infections have devastating health consequences, including infertility, blindness, organ failure, brain damage, birth complications, and in the case of HIV/AIDS, death. Left untreated, gonorrhea and chlamydia can cause pelvic inflammatory disease; a condition relatively common among Black women, and one which renders at least 100,000 women in the United States infertile each year. Syphilis infections during pregnancy pose grave consequences to fetal health—including eye problems, neurological complications, pneumonia, birth defects—and they increase the likelihood of stillbirth or death soon after birth. Finally, Black women afflicted by other STIs are also at disproportionate risk of acquiring HIV, with HIV/AIDS currently the leading cause of death for Black women aged 25-44 years. While Black women account for only 13% of the women in the United States, they account for 57% of all new HIV cases among women in the nation. Despite advances in detection and treatment, however, research has failed to address the multitude of economic and social factors contributing to this problem that costs the U.S. healthcare system $16.4 billion annually.

THE RESEARCH EVIDENCE

Economic and social forces greatly influence the distribution of sexually transmitted infections by affecting behaviors, sexual networks and the likelihood of exposure to infection. However, individual behaviors seem to be the least influential of the three factors. Increasing evidence demonstrates that Black women typically acquire STIs and HIV through lower risk behaviors than White women. Instead, these women tend to acquire the diseases through a complex web of social factors—poverty, residential segregation, excessive institutionalization, and stigma—that affects their sexual networks and exposure to risk.

Poverty heavily influences sexual network patterns and disease infection rates in Black communities, partially through its relationship with violence, intravenous drug use, and trading sex for survival needs. Poverty is also associated with low marriage rates, and unmarried people are more likely to have multiple, concurrent partners compared to married people. Throughout the United States, *residential segregation* further concentrates these effects of poverty and the depth of STI/HIV risk exposure in the community, while it simultaneously limits Black women's access to resources. Compared to other citizens, Blacks are likely to live in areas with low overall health-care quality. The inability to seek medical care for ill health directly contributes to higher levels of disease, as well as continued ease of transmission (through higher viral loads) within the Black community itself. Thus, compared to White women, Black women have an increased likelihood of acquiring STI/HIV from a high-risk, partner, but less access to diagnosis, management and treatment.

Furthermore, *high incarceration rates* of their partners introduce Black women to many risks. Nearly one in every seven young Black men is incarcerated, and Black women largely limit their sexual partners to Black men. In addition to physically removing people from intimate partnerships (and increasing the likelihood of women seeking additional partners), during incarceration men can be introduced to high risk sexual partners and intravenous drug use. They also may forge new long terms links with higher risk groups (e.g. gangs) that continue after exit from jail. Upon return to the community, these men indirectly expose low-risk women in their sexual network to these high risk groups.

The incarceration of large numbers of men can affect a woman even if her specific partner is not incarcerated. This extensive institutionalization has contributed to women outnumbering men in Black communities. In areas with high incarceration and institutionalization rates, the resultant shortage of available, acceptable partners limits Black women's power to negotiate safe sexual behaviors such as condom use. The stereotypes about sexual behaviors within prison also exacerbate the *stigma and conspiracy theories* that permeate Black communities. Due to various factors including a history of homophobia and the unethical treatment of minorities in government, medical and research practices, there is a great deal of silence and inaction around screening and treatment of STIs in the Black population. These factors serve to maintain a core, high risk pool of individuals because participating in preventive behaviors associated with STIs carries the label—for themselves or their partners—of homosexual, unfaithful, or guinea pig.

RECOMMENDATIONS AND SOLUTIONS

Melinda Gates has proposed a three-step model for affecting change within marginalized populations. This type of population-based model is more applicable than individual-level, behavioral interventions because, as noted above, the core causes of sexually transmitted infections among Black women primarily lie at the relational and societal levels. Thus, we use her three categories to propose initiatives to alleviate Black women's disproportionate burden of STIs:

1. Collect and apply real-time data.
2. Distribute prevention and treatment programs to the most at-risk populations.
3. Increase demand for (and thereby use of) sexual health services.

Collect real-time data and apply it to intervention/prevention efforts.

Timely, evidence-based information is an important factor in restricting any infectious disease transmission. Recent studies suggest several ways to better integrate empirical information into prevention and intervention efforts. Real-time evidence that takes structural inequality based on race or gender into account is most relevant to efforts focusing young Black women. For example:

- Focusing on risk behavior alone does not explain why some persons and communities continue to be infected with HIV and other sexually transmitted infections (STIs) more than others. Cluster detection analysis is an approach to prevention which examines how the risk of HIV/STI acquisition differs, or clusters, across groups with similar characteristics. This is an efficient, cost effective, technique to target prevention and intervention efforts to a core group of individuals likely to acquire and transmit STIs. Public health agencies should implement cluster detection analysis to identify sexual networks as starting points for population specific screening efforts.

- Integrating geographic prevalence in the male population (not racial attributes) into STI selective screening criteria substantially increases the efficiency and accuracy of detection among women. When practitioners include geography in selective screening practices, very slight increases in the number of women tested (5%-11%) result in a significantly larger proportion of STI cases identified. (Although including race in the screening criteria has similar effects it should be avoided because it could lead to stigmatization and could amplify the Black population's current distrust of medical practices).

- Collecting blood-based viral load levels (not semen-based) is especially informative about the probability of HIV and hepatitis transmission through vaginal intercourse. Some academic and public discussions have dismissed the evidence regarding blood-based tests because it is not applicable to the men having sex with men population. However, vaginal transmission is an important issue for Black women; and using blood-based viral load information to target services to individuals who are at or above detectable levels could reduce the risk of transmission to these women.

Distribute prevention and treatment services within peoples' lived contexts.

Access to services is often gauged by the physical location of programs. However, the presence or absence of screening and treatment facilities represents only the most basic criteria for determining accessibility and usability. To be effective, programs and services need to be comprehensive, convenient and practical, and should be located throughout the span of the community's reach. Hence, to distribute services appropriately to Black women and their partners, two things must occur:

- Fully funded treatment clinics in areas of concentrated disadvantage must offer comprehensive services. The high rate of STIs among Black women occurs at the nexus of a variety of social forces. In addition to offering sexual health services, evidence from woman-focused HIV interventions suggests that it is imperative for these clinics to provide services that address the social contexts leading to sexual risk behavior, such as sexual negotiation skill building, increasing access to adequate housing, childcare and job training, as well as reducing intimate partner violence.

- Services must be located within the reach of sexual network members who are temporarily displaced, especially in prisons and shelters. Black women largely restrict their sexual partnerships to Black men, and young Black men are overrepresented in prisons and homeless shelters. Therefore, Black women's increased risk of infection cannot be addressed without offering screening and treatment services in men's prisons and men's shelters.

Increase the Demand for STI screening and treatment within the black population.

Partially due to highly visible historic (e.g. the Tuskegee Syphilis Study) and current practices, there is significant mistrust of medical and government intervention in the Black population. For example, in a recent national study, 2 out of every 5 Black adults believed that people who take new HIV medications are "human guinea pigs for the government." These types of views decrease Black women's willingness to seek STI screening and treatment. Practitioners and policy makers can increase demand by:

- Funding information and risk reduction campaigns designed by trusted and recognizable Black entities. Government organizations interested in affecting change among Black women should look to long-standing and trusted Black institutions like the Rainbow Coalition, NAACP, Urban League, and Black National Congress to create, shape, and distribute information and services. Program materials should be associated with recognizable, high profile individuals in these organizations, and should be free of government agency signage.

- Including STI screening as a standard part of women's annual health exams. Women and practitioners alike tend to view sexual health and general women's health services separately. Instead, STI screening should be likened to mammograms and pap smears. STI screening should be on Black women's annual calendar and should be scheduled along with their annual exam. Efforts should aim not only to educate practitioners and health educators to include STI/HIV screening and testing as part of routine care, but to routinize screening such that women are empowered to request it when it is not offered or suggested by their physician.

- Expanding the focus of successful HIV/AIDS de-stigmatization efforts to include general STIs. Organizations such as Greater than AIDS, LIFE AIDS, and Trump AIDS have successfully associated HIV/AIDS treatment with positive aspects of Black culture and desirable, hopeful futures. Yet, many of these efforts do not specifically address other STIs, such as gonorrhea or syphilis, which affect many more Black women and can lead to infertility and even death. These programs should expand their efforts to de-stigmatize general STI testing, educating Black women about the importance of detection and successful treatment as a gateway to a fulfilling life.

In sum, we know that social inequality—poverty, physical and social segregation, high incarceration rates, and limited access to and usability of health care—is the core cause of the elevated prevalence of STIs among Black women. However, there are steps we can take to alleviate the more proximate causes of the disparities. Efforts to effect change among Black women have to include initiatives that reflect their lived reality. Furthermore, they should focus on population and community-level initiatives rather than individual-level or behavioral interventions.

KEY RESOURCES

Adimora, Adaora A., Victor J. Schoenbach, and Irene A. Doherty. 2006. "HIV and African Americans in the Southern United States: Sexual Networks and Social Context." *Sexually Transmitted Diseases* 33(7):S39-S45.

Aral, Sevgi O., Adaora A. Adimora, and Kevin A. Fenton. 2008. "Understanding and Responding to Disparities in HIV and Other Sexually Transmitted Infections in African Americans." *The Lancet* 372(9635):337-40.

Bird, Sheryl T., and Laura M. Bogart. 2005. "Conspiracy Beliefs About HIV/AIDS and Birth Control Among African Americans: Implications for the Prevention of HIV, Other STIs, and Unintended Pregnancy." *Journal of Social Issues* 61(1):109-26.

Crepaz, Nicole, Khiya J. Marshall, Latrina W. Aupont, Elizabeth D. Jacobs, Yuko Mizuno, Linda S. Kay, Patricia Jones, Donna Hubbard McCree, and Ann O'Leary. 2009. "The Efficacy of HIV/STI Behavioral Interventions for African American Females in the United States: A Meta-Analysis." *American Journal of Public Health* 99(11):2069-78.

El-Bassel, Nabila, Nathilee A. Caldeira, Lesia M. Ruglass, and Louisa Gilbert. 2009. "Addressing the Unique Needs of African American Women in HIV Prevention." *American Journal of Public Health* 99(6):996-1001.

Jennings, Jacky M., Frank C. Curriero, David Celentano, and Jonathan M. Ellen. 2005. "Geographic Identification of High Gonorrhea Transmission Areas in Baltimore, Maryland." *American Journal of Epidemiology* 161(1):73-80.

Laumann, Edward O., and Yoosik Youm. 1999. "Racial/Ethnic Group Differences in the Prevalence of Sexually Transmitted Diseases in the United States: A Network Explanation." *Sexually Transmitted Diseases* 26(5):250-61.

Thomas, James C., Brooke A. Levandowski, Malika R. Isler, Elizabeth Torrone, and George Wilson. 2008. "Incarceration and Sexually Transmitted Infections: A Neighborhood Perspective." *Journal of Urban Health* 85(1):90-99.

Wingood, Gina M. and Ralph J. DiClemente. 2000. "Application of the

Theory of Gender and Power to Examine HIV-related Exposures, Risk Factors and Effective Interventions for Women." *Health Education and Behavior* 27(5):539-65.

Wolfe, William A. 2003. "Overlooked Role of African-American Males' Hypermasculinity in the Epidemic of Unintended Pregnancies and HIV/AIDS Cases with Young African-American Women." *Journal of the National Medical Association* 95(9):846-52.

ABOUT THE AUTHORS

Tamara G.J. Leech, Ph.D. is Assistant Professor in the Department of Sociology and Director of the Survey Research Center at Indiana University-Purdue University, Indianapolis. Her scholarship examines Black urban youths' health behaviors—particularly violence and risky sexual behaviors—at the intersection of gender and neighborhood contexts. Dr. Leech's research has been funded by the Robert Wood Johnson Foundation, Woodrow Wilson National Fellowship Foundation, and Indiana Department of Health Maternal and Child Health Division. Direct correspondence to: Tamara G.J. Leech, 303E Cavanaugh Hall, 425 University Blvd., Indianapolis, IN 46208 or tleech@iupui.edu.

Devon J. Hensel, Ph.D. is Assistant Professor of Pediatrics at Indiana University School of Medicine and Assistant Professor of Sociology at Indiana University Purdue University-Indianapolis. Dr. Hensel has a broad background in behavioral science, research methods, complex and longitudinal data analysis, as well as clinical research study design and management. Substantively, her research interests focus on understanding the role of interpersonal factors in the event-level and longitudinal patterns associated with sexual and prevention behavior and STI incidence, as well as understanding the role of sexual partners in dyadic sexual processes.

CHAPTER 6

PROMOTING DIGITAL EQUALITY: THE INTERNET AS A PUBLIC GOOD AND COMMONS

Jason Smith
George Mason University

Preston Rhea
New America Foundation, Open Technology Institute

Sascha Meinrath
New America Foundation, Open Technology Institute

THE PROBLEM

The myriad barriers to access and adoption of affordable, fast broadband internet are causing digital inequalities across contemporary America. This, in turn presents a host of growing social problems, especially for rural and low-income urban communities, especially since the means to learn and participate in society are increasingly becoming mediated through online outlets.

Since the 2005 Supreme Court ruling upholding the Federal Communications Commission's (FCC) decision that broadband cable companies are exempt from common-carrier regulations, the internet service provision sector has become less competitive and more vertically integrated. Increasing capital expenses for building of new infrastructure have raised the bar for new market entrants at the same time that wire line and wireless services have become the key means for modern communications. Proponents of market concentration cite the economies of scale and efficiencies of resource use (e.g., broadcast spectrum, dark fiber) as well as expressing faith that a free market economy is preferable to government regulation. However, the large numbers of Americans who lack internet access, and the high prices and slow speeds of internet access when it is available, raise serious questions about the sense of relying on market forces alone. A growing canon of research reveals an increasingly media-penetrated society where businesses and services are most-used by online consumers. As boundaries among individuals' lives and the media are blurred, communities that lack broad and meaningful internet adoption face multiplying limitations.

Implementing an agenda for digital equality requires policymakers to think of internet access in new ways: we must conceive of the internet as a public good – just as essential as access to affordable housing and health care – in which all people have the right and the reasonable means to participate. Additionally, the internet is a vast commons – a space for creative knowledge and culture to form, grow, and become the building blocks for future cultural products and democratic deliberation.

Two fundamental drivers of broadband adoption are the salience of connectivity to a community's needs and that constituency's ability to use online resources to engage in local issues. However, affordable broadband expansion, although necessary, is not enough on its own to drive digital equality in rural and low-income urban areas. Consider what Losey and Meinrath, in a 2011 *Slate* article, term "the Internet craftsman—the individual who is free to develop networks, services, and applications and who shapes networking technologies better to meet her own needs and those of her community." She constructs and innovates alternative methods of internet connectivity, and it is these Internet craftsmen that policymakers and the public should support as they implement a digital equality agenda.

RESEARCH EVIDENCE

The lack of sufficient broadband infrastructure takes a heavy toll on those living in rural and low-income urban areas. However, focusing solely on access is too narrow and leads to short-sighted policies. Following the turn of the millennium, contemporary research on digital inequality highlighted the limitations of only focusing on the "digital divide" – the difference in access levels different groups faced – and stated that more attention should be paid to the difference in returned gain that people experience from using the internet.

Research shows that digital inequality correlates with key economic, political, and cultural variables – all of which play an important role in the utilization of internet and the gains that can be achieved from it. As a 2010 report from the Pew Research Center's Internet and American Life Project noted, higher-income households (earning over $75,000 annually) were significantly more likely to use internet and email than those in lower-income brackets. These higher-income households were able to maximize their internet use by accessing news online, researching products and other economic outcomes (participating in "e-commerce"), and seeking out health-related information online. Likewise, as current sociological research demonstrates, internet users increasingly adapt their online activities to better manage their everyday lives. The use of the internet to build and maintain social ties (and the capital gains associated with those ties) is found throughout such research.

The lack of meaningful competition in the broadband service market has resulted in service pricing in the United States that far exceeds other developed countries. While rural areas stand at the top of the list for lack of access, over-pricing significantly affects the adoption of broadband for low-income urban areas. Beyond telecommunication firms, larger systemic issues contribute to digital inequality as well. Years of deferred maintenance has resulted in dilapidated broadband infrastructure and cost is cited as the number one reason low-income communities do not adopt broadband – both problems stemming from the lack of checks and balances protecting consumers from corporate profit-seeking – and this, in turn has profound impacts on how we can communicate in the modern world.

Although recent survey research has documented an increase in internet access for low-income urban areas through the use of mobile devices, the ability for users to effectively utilize the internet to capture both capital and social gains is largely limited by the network providers upon which they are dependent. The baseline cost of service that limits home broadband adoption also impacts wireless service provision. While mobile devices let individuals check online news and connect with others, they are increasingly limited by "datacaps" (set amounts of downloadable data), the degradation or blocking of services and applications by wireless providers who demand the right to "reasonable network management," and the high cost of "tethering" (using their phone to connect a separate device to the internet) that keep customers from having full use of the internet.

RECOMMENDATIONS AND SOLUTIONS

Promoting digital equality for the future requires a holistic approach that implements multiple solutions from multiple agents and can foster meaningful and unrestricted internet use and development.

First, people need agency to solve their own problems - economic, social and political. **To extend personal agency to communicating effectively, we must rethink of the internet as a *public good.*** The internet should be viewed as a non-competitive and non-excludable good which is used by a diverse array of actors. To take full advantage of this public good, it must be maintained to be useful to its participants and free from digital enclosures. Maintaining adequate service provision will require substantial further investment in broadband infrastructure as well as development of an ecosystem of ownership models that will provide access that best serves local community needs.

The needs of underserved communities in politics, the media, culture and the economy are too often subjugated to the vagaries and epic failures of market forces (e.g., the current mortgage crisis, Gulf Coast oil spill, telecommunications pricing and speeds). Innovative and meaningful participation on the internet is only possible when individuals are free to actively take part. Meanwhile, myriad new digital divides threaten to prevent the traditionally marginalized and voiceless from telling their own stories. The internet has the potential to generate a culture of digital justice that empowers individuals to share skills and resources to solve their problems. But this potential is undermined when a community-centric, justice-minded agenda is subjugated wholly to centralized, command-and-control infrastructure and business models.

Second, **understanding the internet as a *commons* would foster community growth and strengthen social bonds at the local level**. People can literally build the internet by organizing community-controlled infrastructure. Incumbent service providers stifle this key feature of user-led expansion of the global internet by discouraging community build-out with restrictive end-user acceptable use policies. This risks turning the internet commons into a "pay for play" individual-access model – ignoring the potential universal benefits of network effects in favor of maximizing revenue for an ever-decreasing number of internet service providers. To reclaim the right to communicate, free of the limitations service providers mandate, communities and individuals alike must have the option to build their own channels of communication in a way that is most appropriate to their situation. This approach, which rejects sole reliance upon traditional command-and-control network build-out, is actually far more in keeping with the traditional (decentralized) model that so successfully created the internet in the first place.

One key exemplar of this new thinking is wireless mesh networking, which allows users to connect directly to each other and facilitates the growth of distributed network infrastructures. Mesh wireless networks also provide multiple paths for communication (like a spider web) instead of routing traffic through a central hub, as is normal with cell tower-based networks. With existing freely-available open source tools, communities can build a mesh network with a diverse set of hardware – from high-end carrier-class equipment to familiar off-the-shelf in-home routers, existing computers and laptops, to common mobile devices. The result is a device-as-infrastructure network model inherently supporting peer-to-peer communication while avoiding the path dependencies and vendor lock-in that so often occur with proprietary solutions. More importantly, because the costs associated with open source mesh wireless are often an order of magnitude lower, they can have profound impacts on service level pricing, average return per user, and returns on investment – creating sustainable business models where traditional network architecture and technologies haven't worked previously.

A community mesh network, in fact, counts shared internet bandwidth as only one key service. Any number of applications can "live" on the local network – regardless of whether internet connectivity exists. These services and applications can include high definition video chat, media recording and streaming, hyper-local community radio, businesses and community anchor institutions using router splash pages as electronic billboards, environmental and health alerts and information, multipurpose sensor networks, and even local games and search databases. And since they're all hosted locally, access costs are marginal expenses. Neighborhoods and communities can negotiate directly with one another how their networks interconnect and support each other while maintaining their local social benefits. In this way, communities can capture the value of the internet commons that is often external to the cost-benefit analyses of traditional internet service providers.

Adoption of such frameworks requires multiple policy solutions from multiple agents and active involvement at various levels of government, schools, non-governmental organizations, community anchor institutions, businesses and community organizations. The following are recommendations for these various groups in the promotion of digital equality.

Generally

- Design and implementation choices should make the network open, interoperable and easily extensible and not rely on a central authority to grant permission to use and expand the network.

- Make participatory design of the network and digital literacy through popular education a part of the implementation plan.

- Key decision-makers should explore and invest in alternatives to traditional broadband business models and ensure that underserved communities have the same meaningful access and adoption opportunities enjoyed by the digital-haves.

- The network should be designed to fit the community's existing social networks and goals, not the other way around.

- True two-way communication should be emphasized by aiming for equal upload and download speeds (i.e., speed symmetry).

Policymakers

- The language and concepts used to define the state of broadband penetration, which currently refers to "access" to broadband instead of actual adoption and utilization rates, should be re-examined.

- The federal government must also provide funds and implement educational programs supporting digital literacy.

- State and municipal governments can promote intercity fiber peering and generate programs for small businesses to leverage the value of broadband infrastructure.

- Hold telecommunication firms accountable for broadband infrastructure and for reinvesting profits in expanding affordable broadband access.

- Governments should provide open access fiber to fuel the growing need for bandwidth.

Community-Based Organizations

- Organizations working with underserved constituencies should seek funds to build networks that meet local needs.

- Communities and key leaders at the local level should prioritize the principles of a public good when defining their vision for supporting contemporary communications infrastructures.

- Invest in research and discussions with their constituencies on the importance of internet adoption and utilization and its relation to improving one's life.

- Most importantly, communities should *give building their own communications infrastructure a try*, and not wait for a prescriptive policy solution.

If these principles are soundly incorporated into policy at multiple levels, they will provide a sound basis for protecting open communication and inoculating against censorship and discrimination. As FCC Commissioner Michael Copps is fond of saying, "There's an old Washington axiom: decisions made without you are decisions made against you." Finally, the lessons learned from these design and implementation processes can help prepare communities to provide meaningful input when governments consider future broadband policies – creating a cycle of constructive feedback that will further improve national policy-making for generations to come.

KEY RESOURCES

DiMaggio, Paul, Eszter Hargittai, Coral Celeste, and Steven Shafer. 2004. "From Unequal Access to Differentiated Use: A Literature Review and Agenda for Research on the Digital Divide," in *Social Inequality*, edited by K. Neckerman. New York, NY: Russell Sage Foundation. Pp.355-400.

Fuchs, Christian. 2009. "The Role of Income Inequality in a Multivariate Cross-National Analysis of the Digital Divide." *Social Science Computer Review*, 27(1):41-58.

Losey, James and Sascha Meinrath. 2011. "In Defense of the Internet Crafstman: Universal broadband should be about control, not just access." *Slate*, August 15. http://www.slate.com/articles/technology/future_tense/2011/08/in_defe nse_of_the_internet_craftsman.html

Meinrath, Sascha, James Losey, and Benjamin Lennett. 2011. "A Growing Digital Divide: Internet Freedom and the Negative Impact of Command-and-Control Networking." *IEEE Internet Computing*, July/August:75-79.

Meinrath, Sascha, James W. Losey, and Victor W. Pickard. 2011. "Digital Feudalism: Enclosures and Erasures from Digital Rights Management to the Digital Divide." *CommLaw Conspectus*, 19(2):423-479.

Middleton, Catherine A. and Jock Given. 2011. "The Next Broadband Challenge: Wireless." *Journal of Information Policy*, 1:36-56.

Noam, Eli M. 2009. *Media Ownership and Concentration in America*. New York, NY: Oxford University Press.

No Author. 2005. "Supreme Court Upholds FCC Ruling in *Brand X* Case." *The Computer & Internet Lawyer*, 22(9):32-34.

Schiller, Dan. 1999. *Digital Capitalism: Networking the Global Market System*. Cambridge, MA: MIT Press.

Schradie, Jen. 2011. "The Digital Production Gap: The Digital Divide and Web 2.0 Collide." *Poetics*, 39(2):145-168.

Stern, Michael J., Alison E. Adams, and Shaun Elsasser. 2009. "Digital Inequality and Place: The Effects of Technological Diffusion on Internet Proficiency and Usage across Rural, Suburban, and Urban Counties." *Sociological Inquiry*, 79(4):391-417.

Online Resources

National Alliance for Media Art + Culture: http://www.namac.org/

Open Technology Institute, New America Foundation:
http://oti.newamerica.net/

Pew Research Center's Internet and American Life Project:
http://pewinternet.org

ABOUT THE AUTHORS

Jason Smith (jsm5@gmu.edu) is a Ph.D. student in the Public Sociology program at George Mason University, whose research focuses on access and representation in the media landscape. In 2011, he served as a COMPASS Fellow with New America Foundation's Media Policy Initiative, involved in projects that looked at media policy, the state of journalism, and diversity in media ecosystems.

Preston Rhea is a Program Associate for the Open Technology Institute of the New America Foundation. He organizes community mesh wireless networks in DC, and supports digital justice with research and analysis on community technology. Preston holds a Bachelor of Science degree in electrical engineering from the Georgia Institute of Technology, and spent five years in several countries working with the global student-run organization AIESEC as a local committee co-founder and president, conference organizer and facilitator. He blogs at www.prestonrhea.org.

Sascha Meinrath is the Director of the New America Foundation's Open Technology Institute and is a well-known expert on community wireless networks, open technology, and telecommunications policy. Sascha is the founder of the Commotion ("Internet-in-a-Suitcase") Wireless Project and the co-founder of MeasurementLab.net, a distributed server platform for researchers around the world to deploy Internet measurement tools, advance network research, and empower the public with useful information about their broadband connections. He blogs regularly at www.saschameinrath.com.

CHAPTER 7

U.S. IMMIGRATION LAW, IMMIGRANT ILLEGALITY, AND IMMIGRATION REFORM

Cecilia Menjívar, Ph.D.
Arizona State University

THE ISSUE

The media today are saturated with stories about immigration. There are accounts of immigrants being deported, of workplace raids, of children and parents being separated for uncertain periods of time, of immigrants taking jobs away from Americans, and of immigrants utilizing social services in higher or lower rates than other groups. Such stories fuel the debate about immigration and increase tensions, leading to heated arguments about birthright citizenship and open the way to contemplate solutions that include massive deportations. Missing from all this is an informed understanding of how current US immigration law is structured and how the immigration bureaucracy works on the ground, both of which affect profoundly how legal statuses are created, how immigrants go through the system, and what their actual chances are, in today's system, to live in the country legally.

An important component in this discussion is how immigration law is created and implemented and the consequences this has for how immigrants navigate the system. A focus on the law, how it is created, interpreted, and implemented—and away from the individuals who are categorized and classified into different categories—can bring light to an angle largely missing from the immigration debate but that is crucial for serious conversations about reform. Thus, for instance, there is much discussion in the context of immigration reform about providing or denying a "path to citizenship" to undocumented immigrants currently in the country. However, given immigration laws, technicalities, and the implementation of the law today, this "path" can be bumpy, full of detours, and sometimes even dead ends, making the entire process extremely lengthy and uncertain. But little is known about this process, and it is this lack of information that tends to muddle the discussion, simplify the issue, and prevent serious efforts to propose reasonable reforms to the immigration system.

In this chapter I focus on how contemporary federal immigration law (not state or local level laws and ordinances) and border policies have set the conditions for the increased numbers of undocumented immigrants currently in the country, how their criminalization feeds uninformed debates, and whether the current system offers any real options for legalization. This focus leads naturally to concrete recommendations for policy.

THE RESEARCH EVIDENCE

There are two interconnected aspects of current immigration in the United States that are deeply linked to its system of laws: the number of undocumented immigrants in the country and the deportations of hundreds of thousands each year. The number of undocumented in the country increased rapidly in the 1990s, but has stabilized in recent years; it was estimated at approximately 11 million in 2008. In addition, the number of deportations, which have increased every year, reached close to 400,000 in 2010, a historical high. Whereas reasons for US-bound migration range from economic and educational opportunities in the United States to family reunification and escaping various forms of violence in sending countries, current border policies and immigration laws have been identified as directly affecting the number of immigrants with irregular statuses in the country today as well as the historically high numbers of deportations. For instance, the increased policing of the southern U.S. border has made the journey treacherous and ever more costly physically and financially. Thus, increasing numbers of immigrants who used to engage in circular migration prior to the tightening of the border now stay put in the United States, and in this way avoid risking their lives when crossing and escape the paralyzing debt that accrues to repeat crossers.

In addition to significant modifications in border policy, other changes in immigration law, particularly those instituted with the passing of the Illegal Immigration Reform and Immigrant Responsibility Act of 1996, have closed off paths previously available for undocumented immigrants in the country to regularize their statuses. Today, immigrants who overstay their visas between 180 and 365 days and leave the country are inadmissible (and cannot return legally) for 3 years; those who have overstayed their visas for more than one year are barred from admissibility for 10 years. Furthermore, a provision in the law (Section 245i) that previously allowed certain undocumented immigrants in the country to file for an adjustment of status if they fulfilled other requirements including a petition from family or an

employer and the payment of a fee, was eliminated in 2001. Given this new
legal scenario, immigrants who have overstayed their visas but who live
with their families, work, and are rooted in their communities in the United
States, see little sense in leaving the country. Not knowing when or if they
will ever return, these measures push people to stay put, as these bars are
triggered when individuals leave the country. This is a salient example of
how changes in the law have directly contributed to increasing the number
of undocumented immigrants in the country today.

IIRIRA 1996 also has created avenues for the escalation of enforcement of
the law inside the country (away from the geographic border) in ways that
increasingly criminalize the presence of undocumented immigrants, or of
immigrants who are in the process of regularizing their statuses. In addition
to the 3 or 10 years bar from admissibility, two other provisions in IIRIRA
1996 have shaped the situation we see today: the removal of permanent
legal residents who have ever committed a crime (the law is retroactive) for
which they were sentenced for one year or longer (and have already served
their terms), and the creation of the 287(g) program that authorizes federal
and local law enforcement to enter into agreements to allow officers to
perform immigration enforcement functions. The barring of immigrants
from admissibility and re-entry and the removal of permanent legal
residents (the first law of its kind in the United States) are the twin
provisions encoded in immigration law today that are behind the uncertain
and lengthy separations of families through deportation. And whereas the
287(g) program was created with the intention to catch criminal immigrants
(and it is a voluntary program for municipalities across the country to
implement), it has cast a broader net and many undocumented immigrants
with either no criminal records or with only minor infractions have been
apprehended and deported. This program created the basis for many of the
deportations depicted in the news, and it also contributed to cementing
images of immigrants as criminals, with negative consequences for inflamed
debates about immigration. In addition, in contrast to the Bush
administration's strategy of removing workers through the highly visible
(and media attractive) workplace raids, the Obama administration's quieter
policy of auditing companies to force them to fire workers suspected of
being in the country undocumented is triggering the exit of these workers
who either return to their origin countries (or "self deport") or relocate to

other states. This new approach is seen as more effective in removing undocumented immigrants, since many more workers are eliminated from payrolls—not only those who happened to be at work during a roundup—and it does not attract much attention and potential concerns for workers' rights and opposition.

Another factor that directly influences the number of undocumented immigrants in the country is related to how the law is implemented. With increased attention to the border as a national security concern and with more resources dedicated to 'stem the flow' at the border, the service side of the immigration bureaucracy has lost a considerable amount of resources. The reduced resources in this component of the immigration bureaucracy means that there are fewer officers evaluating applications, fewer judges hearing cases, and fewer individuals doing the routine tasks required to keep the system functioning smoothly. This situation has led to an ever-larger number of backlogged applications, particularly from the largest sending countries, and mostly in the family reunification category, the largest avenue for immigrants to gain admission lawfully in the United States. All this translates on the ground in applications often taking years to process, petitions for certain provisions easily taking a decade to be adjudicated, and even a simple change of address form taking a year or more to be processed. In the meantime, the immigrants whose applications have been submitted exist for years in "limbo" as they wait and hope for a successful verdict, while at the same time remaining in the 'undocumented' category because technically they are not yet permanent legal residents.

Furthermore, in a recent reversal in federal policy, starting in the second half of 2011, immigration authorities have been instructed to not bring criminal charges to undocumented immigrant workers who have no criminal records. In an effort to focus on the criminals among these immigrants and thus to keep with the objective of securing the nation, non-criminal undocumented immigrants will not be rounded up and deported massively. However, this does not mean that these immigrants will receive a reprieve or that a path to legalization will be created for them; they will remain undocumented and working under increasingly worse conditions (as employers fire them in order to comply with the federal audits), barred from most forms of public assistance, and unable to travel outside the country. This action on the part of the federal government might have the additional unintended consequence of expanding the undocumented population, as these individuals will live in "legal limbo": not deported but not extended opportunities for legalization either. While welcoming the opportunity not to be deported, without regular status (i.e., permanent legal residence), technically, they are counted as undocumented.

The backlogs of applications are not evenly divided across all countries of origin, or for all admission categories. Even though the family reunification category accounts for approximately two thirds of all legal admissions, the current system that sets a limit of 20,000 visas to each country annually, contributes to longer backlogs for particular countries that for historical reasons send more immigrants to the United States. Thus, for instance, for Mexico and the Philippines family reunification visas account for about 90 percent and 75 percent of all entries, respectively. And for these countries the backlog in the various family categories is particularly long; for instance, it takes approximately 21 years for the sibling of a Mexican petitioner to enter the United States, and 19 years for the sibling of a Filipino petitioner.

Importantly, these backlogs affect even legislation specifically created to help vulnerable groups. For instance, women applying to regularize their status under the Violence against Women Act (VAWA) often go through the same arduous and lengthy process as immigrants applying under various categories of family reunification. The possibility of waiting for months or years for their applications to be processed often dissuades women in domestic violence situations from applying for protection. Indeed, VAWA applications make it clear how immigrants of different nationalities do not have the same experiences in the application process, as those coming from countries with long backlogs wait longer and face more uncertainty than those coming from countries with shorter backlogs (and thus fewer demands for visas). Thus, the persistence of backlogs for certain groups, those with particular histories of U.S.-bound migration such as Mexico or the Philippines, creates an uneven playing field for applicants of different nationalities.

A key issue missing from public discussions of immigration today is that an individual wishing to immigrate to the United States, or who is already in the country undocumented, must have either an employer willing to sponsor their visa process or a family member willing and able to petition for them to immigrate. Various family categories, such as an immediate relative of a U.S. citizen or the son or daughter of a permanent legal resident, have different waiting times. Requirements to sponsor a relative can be onerous, particularly for immigrant workers who do not have enough resources. Requirements for sponsoring a relative can include letters from the employer of the sponsoring daughter or son, bank statements, a bank letter detailing banking transactions, years of income tax returns, and letters from the consulate, an invitation letter, and proof of relationship to the person being sponsored. An individual who does not have access to either an employer who is willing to go through securing an employment visa or a relative with resources to sponsor them has no possibility to regularize their status under the current system. These immigrants, though more than willing to regularize their status (and to get on the path to citizenship), face a legal dead end. Thus, given the reality of immigration law and border policies described here, it should not come as a surprise that two-thirds of the undocumented immigrants in the United States today have been in the country for more than 10 years, with a full one third having resided in the country for 15 years or longer, most of whom are either waiting for applications to be adjudicated or simply facing legal dead ends.

RECOMMENDATIONS AND SOLUTIONS

Thus, while much attention, discussion, and resources are devoted to border enforcement and security, to the enforcement of the law in the country through workplace inspections and ID checks, and the creation of programs to expel immigrants, a fundamental shift in attention to the service area of the immigration bureaucracy would contribute significantly to moving the conversation forward. This approach would include:

- A substantial increase in funding for the service side of the immigration bureaucracy, so that applications are processed more swiftly and backlogs decreased.

- Unused visa allocations (from the 20,000 country limit) should be transferred to other countries that need them more. For instance, if a country does not use all its 20,000 visas in one year, those spots can be transferred to the countries with the largest backlogs.

- Reinstate the 245i (or the LIFE Act), so that immigrants who are out of status already in the country, and likely already very rooted, can adjust their status and live out of the shadows of the law.

- Eliminate the provision for deportations of permanent legal residents from the IIRIRA 1996, as they have already served their sentences in the United States and deporting them constitutes added punishment.

- Eliminate the 3 or 10 year bars to re-entry, so that undocumented individuals can leave the country if they wish, without fearing the penalty.

- Eliminate agreements for local law enforcement to enforce federal immigration law, so that the criminalization of immigrants we see today is lessened and an environment for serious and constructive discussion is created.

KEY RESOURCES[ii]

Gindling, T.H. and Sara Z. Poggio. 2008. Family Separation and Reunification as a Factor in the Educational Success of Immigrant Children. Maryland Institute for Policy Analysis and Research, University of Maryland. http://www.umbc.edu/economics/wpapers/wp_09_104_FinalReport-FamilySeparationandReunification.pdf .

Gonzales, Roberto G. "Learning to Be Illegal: Undocumented Youth and Shifting Legal Contexts in the Transition to Adulthood." *American Sociological Review*, 76 (4): 602-619.

Hagan, Jacqueline, Nestor Rodriguez, and Brianna Castro. 2011. "Social Effects of Mass Deportations by the United States government,

2000-10." *Ethnic and Racial Studies* 34(8):1374-91.

Migration Information Source. 2011. US in Focus.
http://www.migrationinformation.org/USFocus/.

Passel, Jeffrey and D'Vera Cohen. 2011. Unauthorized Immigrant
Population: National and State Trends, 2010. Washington, DC:
Pew Hispanic Center.
http://www.pewhispanic.org/files/2011/12/Unauthorized-
Characteristics.pdf.

ABOUT THE AUTHOR

Cecilia Menjívar, Ph.D. is Cowden Distinguished Professor in the School of Social and Family Dynamics at Arizona State University. Her immigration research has focused on immigrant social networks, gender and generational relations, and religion and the place of the church in individuals' lives. In recent years she has been examining the effects of immigration laws on different aspects of immigrants' lives and on effects of deportation in countries of origin. She is the author of the books, *Fragmented Ties: Salvadoran Immigrant Networks in America* (University of California Press, 2000) and *Enduring Violence: Ladina Women's Lives in Guatemala* (University of California Press, 2011), both winners of several awards, editor of *Through the Eyes of Women: Gender, Social Networks, Family and Structural Change in Latin America and the Caribbean* (De Sitter, 2003), co-editor of *When States Kill: Latin America, the US, and Technologies of Terror* (University of Texas Press, 2005) and of *Latinos/as in the United States: Changing the Face of América* (Springer 2008) and author of numerous refereed journal articles on immigration-related issues.

CHAPTER 8

JOBS FOR AMERICA

Carolyn Cummings Perrucci, Ph.D.
Purdue University

Robert Perrucci, Ph.D.
Purdue University

THE PROBLEM

During the last 30-40 years, the United States has lost millions of jobs as the result of plant closings, shifting investment abroad, downsizing, and outsourcing by many of the country's largest and best-known corporations. Most of these jobs have been in the high-wage unionized manufacturing sector. After World War II, manufacturing, as a share of total U. S. jobs, was at a peak of 40 percent, slipped to 27 percent in 1981, and slipped further to 12 percent in 2005. By 2010, the total loss of manufacturing jobs in the U.S. was between one-fourth and one-third of the peak level of jobs in this sector. This massive job loss has been facilitated by a variety of trade and tax policies endorsed by administrations and Congresses of both Democrats and Republicans. The loss of middle class jobs has been accompanied by declining wages, loss of benefits, and declining job security.

The erosion of the manufacturing sector has been accompanied by the growth of the financial sector as the new producer of wealth, leading many political leaders to believe that as long as the economy was growing it didn't matter whether the growth was coming from producing cars and home appliances or creating new schemes for financial investment. Recent research indicates that when corporations shifted investment from improving current plant and production to investment in the financial sector, there was a decrease in labor's share of corporate income and expansion of investor and executive's share.

The thirty-plus years of chronic job loss and wage stagnation for middle-income blue and white collar workers has been aggravated by the financial crisis of 2008 and the economic recession that followed. As of this writing (December, 2011) there are about 14 million Americans who are unemployed, with millions more part-time workers who are seeking full-time work.

RESEARCH EVIDENCE

Data from the Office of Technology and Department of Labor have documented the extent of job loss beginning in the mid-1970s. Numerous research articles and books have documented job loss and declining wages. Beginning in the mid-1970s and continuing to the present, there has been a steady decline of higher-wage unionized workers in the auto industries, steel mills, rubber plants, and textile mills. The reshaping of the occupational structure continued through the late 1980s to the mid-1990s, when the strategy was expanded to include not only plant closings and relocations but "restructuring and downsizing" as well, often directed at eliminating white-collar jobs. In 2003 and 2004, the corporate strategy of "outsourcing" became the latest approach to eliminating American jobs. Outsourcing involves using the capabilities of the Internet and new telecommunications technology to hire workers in other countries to take over jobs filled formerly by American workers, a practice used extensively in creating overseas customer service call centers and hiring computer programmers to work while remaining in their home countries.

During the 2001-2006 period over 2 million new U.S. jobs were created but that number fell far short of what is needed to keep up with population growth and new entrants into the labor market. Of the new jobs that were created over the past half-decade, most are at lower wages, with fewer benefits, and with less secure job tenure compared to the jobs that were lost. Pay reductions in the last five years occurred even for highly educated workers in high-skill fields, such as software and electrical engineering, marketing, and business administration. The overall effect of these trends has been the imposition of intense pressure by employers on workers, resulting in the lowering of workers' real wages and a substantial weakening of workers' rights and collective bargaining power.

The official unemployment rate provides additional evidence that not everyone is benefiting as corporate profits grow and inflation remains low. The official estimate is based upon a monthly national sample survey of U.S. households, which asks people a series of questions about whether they are currently working or looking for work. Only those who are unemployed, but claim to be actively looking for work, are classified as unemployed. The annual unemployment rate more than doubled from 4.7 percent in 2001 to 9.6 percent a decade later in 2010. The official unemployment rate underestimates actual unemployment because it excludes part-time workers who seek full-time jobs and discouraged workers who have given up looking for work. These "discouraged workers" have stopped looking for work because their experiences tell them the search is pointless. Also excluded are employed part-time workers who want full-time jobs but cannot find them. The official rate also fails to acknowledge that the unemployment rate for different groups of Americans, such as women and minorities, may be double the official rate. Black Americans, for example, typically are unemployed at a rate that is almost double the white rate (16.0 percent vs. 8.7 percent in 2010.) The number of jobless young Black Americans aged 16 to 19 years old in America's cities presents major crises, with an unemployment rate of 43 percent compared with 23.2 percent of young whites.

Unemployment is only part of the picture of the conditions facing most workers in blue collar or non-managerial jobs. Annual hours worked for married men and women increased while income growth declined or remained stagnant. As might be expected, total debt from mortgages, home equity loans, and consumer credit, as a share of annual disposable income, reached its highest level (141 percent) in 2007.

RECOMMENDATIONS AND SOLUTIONS

We offer recommendations and policy initiatives to deal with three jobs-related issues: first, to provide expanded support for the currently unemployed; second, to enact new policies to protect existing jobs; and third, to enact a Federal-State national job-creation program aimed at restoring America's infrastructure.

Support the Unemployed.

Policies to address unemployment should be developed at multiple levels. First, there should be a response to income loss experienced by unemployed workers. The U.S. requires a major policy initiative involving the federal government to improve the amount of unemployment benefits available to displaced workers and to set uniform standards for states to follow to deliver benefits. This should be combined with efforts at the state and local levels to assist the unemployed in obtaining temporary delays in rent or home mortgage payments and utility bills (which account for a sizable proportion of monthly expenses). Given the large number of long-term unemployed, it is important to develop policies to keep unemployed women and men attached to the labor market instead of becoming permanent drop outs. For example, there should be efforts to expand wage subsidy programs that would allow the unemployed to work part time while still receiving unemployment benefits.

A second policy initiative should provide social services to unemployed workers and their families while they are participating in retraining and relocation programs. Local unemployment offices could establish referral relationships between the unemployed workers/families and appropriate agencies and counseling practitioners in the community.

The third policy initiative should focus on stronger legislation to place the human and social costs of unemployment at the center of economic decision-making. Current policy attempts to assist those whose jobs have been moved overseas through the Trade Adjustment Act and Title III of the Job Training and Partnership Act. The former provides some severance and retraining for workers whose unemployment is due to international competition, and the latter provides retraining for workers whose jobs have been eliminated. Studies of the effectiveness of these programs, however, indicate that they serve relatively few displaced workers.

Protect Existing Jobs.

Congress should enact legislation to slow down the flight of jobs and capital by making disinvestment less attractive to corporate decision makers. Legislation should require corporations that close or reduce domestic operations to move jobs abroad to pay for the costs of 1) retraining and educating displaced workers, 2) the repayment of tax abatements and other financial incentives provided to the corporation by the community, and 3) the payment of a tax on corporate profits earned abroad (currently profits earned from overseas operations are not taxed). The collection and disbursement of assessment funds should be the responsibility of an appropriate agency in the Department of Labor.

Create New Jobs for America.

We propose for consideration a stimulus plan that can create jobs for average Americans and can do so in a way that unifies people in a belief that it serves the common good. The focus would be on America's deteriorating infrastructure of interstate highways, state roads, bridges and dams, aviation, drinking water, toxic waste sites, national power grid, public parks, beaches and recreation sites. The American Society of Civil Engineers has provided a Public Infrastructure Report Card of conditions in 15 areas, and the grades have been mediocre to nearly failing for several decades. These projects would not be make-work, but vital for the health and safety of Americans, no matter where they live or how much money they make.

Recent high-profile disasters such as the failure of the levees to protect New Orleans from Katrina and the collapse of a major bridge in Minneapolis provide ample evidence of the need for improving America's infrastructure.

How would Jobs for America work? We believe that the project should be launched initially as a citizen initiative because it projects the idea of shared costs, and it puts additional pressure on elected officials to support the project with the necessary funding. The proposed project will fail unless it has pressure from citizens to create the project and a willingness to join in paying for the project. How would we begin? When Americans file their tax returns each April 15, they would be invited to make a voluntary contribution of $100 to $500 to the project by adding the amount to the tax they owe or deduct their contribution from their tax rebate. If 20 million taxpayers contributed an average of $100 it would generate $2 billion for the project. More than 132 million Americans file tax returns, and we believe that at least 20 million would buy into the project.

The political pressure of a national citizen-led stimulus plan would require Congress to become a partner with citizens' voluntary contributions by providing matching funds of 10 times what citizens contribute; in this example, $20 billion. The money would come from the procurement side of the defense budget (currently at $104 billion) which always has spending for new ships or planes that the military has not requested. It could also come from eliminating "wars of choice" like the 2011 Libyan involvement, estimated to cost between $750 million and $938 million for less than one year of U.S. participation.

Infrastructure building projects would be located in each state, and when states apply for project funds to rebuild infrastructure, they would have to make a matching contribution, either financial or in-kind. National labor unions would help provide the skilled work force of carpenters, electricians and masons that would be at the heart of the infrastructure projects. They would be expected to become a partner by making wage and work rule concessions to help reduce the cost of the infrastructure projects.

The project would be started by bringing together a leadership team of high-profile Americans, such as Bill Gates and Warren Buffet, who are unifying symbols with a record of having worked on behalf of the common good. They would initiate a national public education effort to inform Americans about the Jobs for America project. Buy-in contributions would come from national advertising firms and national media outlets who would work together to deliver the message to the American public.

Once the project is launched through the proposed voluntary contributions at tax time (described above), it would need to be sustained on a continuing basis either by acts of Congress to fund the project or by new taxes. Since infrastructure is a widely shared public good, our proposal includes a plan for shared revenue contributions in the form of targeted taxes to support the project, including: a new targeted jobs tax on high income earners, a targeted wealth tax, a targeted transaction tax for major stock exchanges, a targeted payroll tax on all employees, and a shift of money from the procurement side of the defense budget to the new jobs project. By targeted tax we mean that the new revenue will be used only for the Jobs for America Project and for a specific time period.

 The estimated cost of rebuilding America's entire deteriorating infrastructure contained in the American Society of Civil Engineers report is about $2 trillion over 5 years, or about $400 billion a year. This annual cost may exceed what may be realistic regarding what could be generated from the new taxes described above. It may require selecting those public projects in greatest need of rehabilitation while delaying others. This is a question of what the American people will accept in the form of new taxes to rehabilitate America's infrastructure and employing millions of American workers to do the work.

There is additional potential for the creation of "green jobs" in new production niches in wind, solar, and other sustainable technologies, as long as the production is in U.S.-based industries. One study conducted by the U.S. Green Building Council estimates a potential for 7.9 million jobs in the construction sector between 2009 and 2013. An expanded study of potential growth was funded by Congress in 2010, asking the Bureau of Labor Statistics to develop estimates of potential green job growth across all production sectors.

The solution to the current economic crisis and recession will depend upon a sustained effort to create jobs in a way that calls on all Americans to share the pain and the gain. The key to restoring hope requires a combination of creating jobs and making existing jobs more secure. It is time to bring Americans together for another "moon mission," but this time we should land in the United States.

*

KEY RESOURCES

American Society of Civil Engineers, *Report Card for America's Infrastructure*, *(https://apps.asce.org/reportcard/2009/grades.cfm)*.

Bluestone, Barry and Bennet Harrison. 1982. *The Deindustrialization of America*. New York: Basic Books.

Mishel, Lawrence, Jared Bernstein, and Heidi Shierholz. 2009. *The State of Working America, 2008/2009*. Ithaca New York: Cornell University Press.

Perrucci, Carolyn Cummings and Robert Perrucci. 2008. "Unemployment," *Encyclopedia of the Life Course and Human Development*, Farmington Hills, MI: Gale.

Perrucci, Robert and Carolyn Cummings Perrucci, (eds.). 2007. *The Transformation of Work in the New Economy*. New York: Oxford University Press.

Perrucci, Robert and Earl Wysong. 2008. *The New Class Society: Goodbye American Dream?* New York: Rowman and Littlefield.

Perrucci, Robert and Carolyn Cummings Perrucci. 2009. *America at Risk: The Crisis of Hope, Trust, and Caring*. New York: Rowman and Littlefield.

Reich, Robert. 1983. *The Next American Frontier*. New York: Time Books.

Tomaskovic-Devey, Donald and Ken-Hou Lin. 2011. "Income Dynamics, Economic Rents, and the Financialization of the U.S. Economy." *American Sociological Review*,76: 538-559.

Uchitelle, Louis. 2006. *The Disposable American: Layoffs and Their Consequences*. New York: Knopf, 2006.

ABOUT THE AUTHORS

Carolyn Cumming Perrucci, Ph.D. and **Robert Perrucci, Ph.D.** are Professors of Sociology at Purdue University. Their most recent joint publication is *America at Risk: Crisis of Hope, Trust, and Caring* (Rowman and Littlefield Publishing).

CHAPTER 9

POVERTY, INEQUALITY, AND THE SHREDDED SAFETY NET

Frances Fox Piven, Ph.D.
City University of New York, Graduate Center

THE PROBLEM

Poverty and inequality have risen in the United States at the same time that both safety nets and the minimal ideological foundation undergirding them have been under assault. Early in 2011, the U.S. Census Bureau *reported* that 14.3% of the population, or 47 million people -- one in six Americans -- were living below the official poverty threshold, currently set at $22,400 annually for a family of four. Some 19 million people are living in what is called extreme poverty, which means that their household income falls in the bottom half of those considered to be below the poverty line. More than a third of those extremely poor people are children. Indeed, *more than half* of all children younger than six living with a single mother are poor. Extrapolating from this data, Emily Monea and Isabel Sawhill of the Brookings Institution estimate that *further sharp increases* in both poverty and child poverty rates lie in our American future.

Why? Many blame the impact of globalization and the new economy on the US occupational structure. This is an incomplete diagnosis because it ignores the policy impact on poverty of the corporate "class war" in the United States that began in the 1960's. In fact, class war was the overarching goal of policies that led to a massive shift of the burden of taxation, the cannibalization of government services through privatization, wage cuts and enfeebled unions, and the deregulation of business, banks, and financial institutions. Throughout the decades of corporate aggression, the poor, blacks, and immigrants were an endlessly useful rhetorical foil, a propagandistic distraction used to win elections and make bigger gains. A host of new think tanks, political organizations, and lobbyists in Washington D.C. carried the message that the country's problems were caused by the poor whose shiftlessness, criminal inclinations, and sexual promiscuity were being indulged by a too-generous welfare system.

RESEARCH EVIDENCE

The official numbers actually don't tell the full story. The poverty line is calculated as simply three times the minimal food budget first introduced in 1959, and then adjusted for inflation in food costs. In other words, the American poverty threshold takes no account of the cost of housing or fuel or transportation or health-care costs, all of which are rising more rapidly than the cost of basic foods. So the poverty measure grossly understates the real cost of subsistence.

Moreover, in 2006, interest payments on consumer debt had already put more than four million people, not officially in poverty, below the line, making them *"debt poor."* Similarly, if *childcare costs*, estimated at $5,750 a year in 2006, were deducted from gross income, many more people would be counted as officially poor. Nor are these catastrophic levels of poverty merely a temporary response to rising unemployment rates or reductions in take-home pay resulting from the great economic meltdown of 2008. Poverty was on the rise before the Great Recession hit. Between 2001 and 2007, poverty *actually increased* for the first time on record during an economic recovery, from 11.7% in 2001 to 12.5% in 2007. Poverty rates for single mothers in 2007 were 49% higher in the U.S. than in 15 other high-income countries. Similarly, black employment rates and income were declining *before* the recession struck. The Associated Press recently reported that fully half of all Americans were now either poor or low income, roughly $45,000 for a family of four, according to Census data.

In part, all of this was inevitable fallout from a decades-long effort to reduce labor costs by weakening unions and changing public policies that protected workers and those same unions. As a result, National Labor Board decisions became far less favorable to both workers and unions, workplace regulations were not enforced, and the minimum wage lagged far behind inflation. The overall impact of the campaign to reduce labor's share of national earnings meant that a growing number of Americans couldn't earn even a poverty-level livelihood.

The Great Recession sharply worsened these trends. The Economic Policy Institute reports that the typical working-age household, which had already seen a decline of roughly $2,300 in income between 2000 and 2006, *lost another $2,700* between 2007 and 2009. And when "recovery" arrived, however uncertainly, it was mainly in low-wage industries, which *accounted for* nearly half of what growth there was. Manufacturing continued to contract, while the labor market lost 6.1% of payroll employment. New investment, when it occurred at all, was more likely to be in machinery than in new workers, *so unemployment levels remain alarmingly high*. In other words, the recession accelerated ongoing market trends toward lower-wage and ever more insecure employment.

The recession also prompted further cutbacks in welfare programs. Because cash assistance has become so hard to get, thanks to so-called welfare reform, and fallback state-assistance programs have been crippled, the federal food stamp program has come to carry much of the weight in providing assistance to the poor. Renamed the "Supplemental Nutritional Assistance Program," it was boosted by funds provided in the Recovery Act, and benefits temporarily rose, as did participation. But Congress has repeatedly attempted to slash the program's funds, and even to divert some of the funds into farm subsidies, while efforts, not yet successful, have been made to deny food stamps to any family that includes a worker on strike.

RECOMMENDATIONS AND SOLUTIONS

The fight to re-claim a moral economy has been forcefully articulated by the Occupy Wall Street movement. The rapid spread of occupations means that the message of opposition to corporate control of politics and rising inequality has resonated. Movements have often been crucial vehicles of societal transformations in the past. And it will take an upheaval of historic dimensions to force the reigning financial and business interests and the politicians who kowtow to them to move in new directions, to cede a measure of democratic regulation of finance and business, to give in to policies that empower workers and their unions, to go along with policies that limit the corruption of electoral politics by big money and its propaganda and, not least, to restore and expand the safety net.

It is useful to distinguish between ameliorative policies that have some political traction in the short run, and longer term solutions that promise more significant restructuring of economy and society but seem unfeasible at the moment. In the immediate future we can take a leaf from the proposals of the congressional Progressive Caucus and push for a large economic stimulus program through massive public investment in job creation, for the repair of dilapidated schools, mass transit facilities and public parks, and to complete neighborhood energy efficiency projects. Climate change hovers over us, and yet the U. S. lags behind China in developing green energy and the jobs that would create. We should also work for the protection and expansion of public service employment, for measures at the federal and state level which would put a halt to mass layoffs of teachers, healthcare and childcare workers, and then we should push for the expansion of these badly needed services. We should also support the extension and expansion of existing safety net programs, including benefits for the unemployed, assistance for needy families, food/nutritional subsidies, housing subsidies, nutritional assistance to mothers and infants, and so on. These programs are far from perfect, but they have reduced poverty in the United States, and they have gone far toward softening the blows of an economy in recession. And because union jobs are better jobs, we should fight to shore up the union protections that have been steadily eroded since the initial passage of the National Labor Relations Act.

Over the long run when anything or nothing is possible, we can contemplate far more ambitious and transforming changes that would eliminate poverty, and by doing so increase democracy, in politics and the economy. If our multiple and conditional income support programs were consolidated into one guaranteed income program, that program would gain the broad support of now diverse and fractured constituents, and working people would gain the power of being able to refuse degrading and badly paid work. Experiments in a solidary economy of cooperative enterprises could initiate the long sought possibility of democratically controlled workplaces. And what about the possibility of regulating investment in the interest of a more egalitarian society by nationalizing the banks and taxing speculative transactions? And rolling back campaign spending, especially by fat cats? Or fully enfranchising the citizenry, and ensuring equal representation in the electoral college and the Congress?

The future of the United States is murky and uncertain. It is a frightening moment and inevitably we talk a lot about the calamities that threaten. But there are large possibilities for a better society as well.

KEY RESOURCES[iii]

Piven, Frances Fox and Richard Cloward. 1978. *Poor People's Movements: Why They Succeed, How They Fail.* New York: Vintage.

Piven, Frances Fox. 2011. *Who's Afraid of Frances Fox Piven?: The Essential Writings of the Professor Glenn Beck Loves to Hate.* New York: The New Press.

ABOUT THE AUTHOR

Frances Fox Piven, Ph.D, is Distinguished Professor in Sociology and Political Science at the CUNY Graduate Center. Dr. Piven is an expert in urban politics, voting rights, and the development of the welfare state. Dr. Piven is one of the foremost political sociologists in the country, having written influential work on protest, the welfare state, and voting. Dr. Piven is also a past-president of the American Sociological Association. She is cofounder of Human SERVE (Service Employees Registration and Voter Education), an organization that worked to increase voter registration among underrepresented and low-income populations.

CHAPTER 10

PRESERVING AFFORDABLE HOUSING AND
BUILDING WEALTH IN AN ECONOMIC
RECOVERY:
LIMITED-EQUITY COOPERATIVES AS AN
ALTERNATIVE TO TENANT DISPLACEMENT

John N. Robinson III
Northwestern University

Katie Kerstetter
George Mason University

THE PROBLEM

Amid a worsening housing crisis, major public housing reform policies fail to empower low-income housing residents and weaken the prospects of economic recovery. Limited equity cooperatives provide a promising alternative.

In the past 20 years, more than 200,000 units of public housing have been demolished or lost. Housing subsidy contracts have expired and federal funding has lagged behind what local agencies need to operate and maintain public housing. Government efforts to rehabilitate public housing often has come at the expense of displacing low-income residents, as poverty de-concentration policies have become the centerpiece of public housing reform. According to many policy analysts, public housing can be distinguished from other federal housing programs in that it is a "deep subsidy," that is, an effective buffer against affordable housing loss and displacement. The dismantling of public housing, on the other hand, has not only caused widespread housing instability and displacement, but has also resulted in a net reduction of housing stock, as unit replacement has fallen far short of demolition. Although public housing accounts for a limited but still sizable segment of low-income renters, the more serious consequence of this policy shift is that public housing displacement exacerbates the larger problem of affordable housing loss.

Public housing reform historically has encompassed a broad set of changes in the production and distribution of low-income housing; however, we limit our discussion to the particular family of reform policies most influential in impacting existing public housing since the early 1990s. These policies tend to resemble the HOPE (Homeownership and Opportunity for People Everywhere) VI program, a federal policy initiative enacted in 1992 that offers revitalization and demolition grants to public housing authorities to improve "severely distressed" housing stock, attract new streams of private financing, and "de-concentrate" poverty. Typically, HOPE VI transforms public housing by demolishing projects and erecting low-density, mixed-income, and mixed-finance developments in their place. As stated previously, however, in this paper "HOPE VI-style policies" does not refer to single a policy but rather a family of reform policies using the rationales and instruments detailed above.

We contrast Limited Equity Cooperatives (LECs) with HOPE VI-style policies for two main reasons. First is the significant reach HOPE VI has achieved not only in terms of the number of properties redeveloped but also in terms of its function as a dominant housing reform strategy. Until recently, HOPE VI demolition and redevelopment comprised the single largest poverty de-concentration effort in U.S. housing policy. As the dominant approach to public housing reform at the turn of the 21st century, versions of the HOPE VI model have been adopted by state and local governments as part of their locally-funded affordable housing programs. Second, the HOPE VI program is unique among other approaches to public housing reform in the degree to which it involves involuntary relocation (i.e. displacement). In this paper, we detail the strengths and weaknesses associated with HOPE VI-style policies and describe limited-equity cooperatives (LECs) as an alternative mechanism to preserve affordable housing without displacing tenants.

RESEARCH EVIDENCE

HOPE VI-style policies have proved unsuccessful as strategies of redeveloping and preserving low-income housing for public housing tenants.

HOPE VI-style policies generally present public housing residents with two options. The first is not to move at all: mixed-income approaches are promoted as opportunities for residents to reoccupy newly-redeveloped housing sites. Resettlement into mixed-income housing developments have been associated with many positive outcomes such as: lower poverty rates, higher neighborhood satisfaction, greater informal social control, more access to higher quality services, and a higher quality of life more generally. Indeed, there is no real disagreement among researchers about the positive effects of mixed income housing for residents able to gain occupancy in the newly developed sites. However, although studies have found that residents overwhelmingly wish to return to original sites after redevelopment, this option has been the least available in practice. Redevelopment often reduces the total number of units by 50 percent or more, with only a fraction of remaining units designated as affordable to families from the original development. The undeniable upside to mixed-income policies, then, is limited by the relatively small number of residents that would ever be able to benefit from it.

A more available option has been for tenants to move to new rental housing using Housing Choice Vouchers. A common misconception is that vouchers are more cost effective than the preservation of traditional public housing; studies have shown that vouchers are more expensive when transition costs are considered. Nonetheless, the relocation voucher process accommodates substantially more original public housing families than mixed-income reoccupation and shows some positive outcomes. For example, residents report feeling safer and better appreciating the quality of their new units. In objective measures too, studies have shown improvements in housing as well as neighborhood characteristics. Additionally, when residents have been able to move to more distant, affluent neighborhoods—such as the Gautreaux demonstration and, to a lesser extent, the MTO program—residents have shown notable improvements in education and employment figures. However, these more substantive outcomes have been largely absent in HOPE VI relocation, as residents have generally been relocated to other poor and racially-segregated neighborhoods. Even in terms of sheer housing provision the voucher relocation process has fallen short, as nearly 60 percent of voucher users report having difficulty paying rent or utilities in private rental markets. Where rental markets have been tight, residents have increasingly been re-concentrated into areas of high poverty. Dispersal policies, therefore, can work when residents are able to move further away, or when local housing markets are amenable to large influxes of low-income residents. But these two conditions are rarely met and, consequently, dispersal policies have not done much to improve the quality of life for poor households.

Research evaluating HOPE VI redevelopment tends to highlight what has been discussed above: how mixed-income and dispersal policies impact the housing prospects and well-being of public housing residents. Because policy-makers understand relocation as a strategy to fight concentrated poverty, they assume that residents are automatically better off in more affluent neighborhoods. However, recent research advances a more complicated picture. Dispersal policies separate residents from the informal networks they rely on and uproot the communities they cherish, even as they potentially introduce poor households to more and better quality resources of other neighborhoods. Additionally, recent research shows that poor neighborhoods actually contain *more* formal organizations and establishments on average than their non-poor counterparts. In this way, policies that relocate residents of poor neighborhoods may ultimately move them even *further away* from the organizational resources they need on a daily basis, even if the social capital gained from having more affluent neighbors may potentially make up for this deficit. Perhaps an even more pressing concern, however, is the extent to which major housing reform policies steadily reduce the total stock of low-income housing at a time when it has become increasingly susceptible to the risk of permanent loss. Despite the benefits associated with mixed-income and dispersal policies, we must ask ourselves a tough question: are they worth the tremendous cost of affordable housing loss?

RECOMMENDATIONS AND SOLUTIONS

Limited-equity cooperatives (LECs) provide an alternative mechanism to preserve affordable housing without displacing tenants.

Public housing remains a critical component of our nation's low-income housing supply; limited- equity cooperatives (LECs) offer a way to reform public housing without displacing households or eliminating units. As of 2003, 425,000 limited-equity cooperative units were operating in the U.S. In a typical arrangement, LECs are owned cooperatively by residents. Residents purchase a share in their building and may also make monthly payments that are often well below the market rent for the surrounding neighborhood. As cooperative members, residents are responsible for the day-to-day management and governance of their building. Many LECs balance these responsibilities by electing residents to a governing board and hiring an outside company to manage the building. Nonprofit entities (e.g. a local government, land trust, or nonprofit) often help with the financing and development of LECs as well as the provision of financial and management training for residents.

To maintain affordability, LEC charters generally place two restrictions on their residents. The first, a prohibition on the sale of the building to private developers, is intended to maintain the long-term affordability of the LEC building. The second, a limitation on the amount of equity individual owners are able to realize at resale, ensures that individual units will remain affordable. When residents sell their share in the LEC, they receive what they invested in their property plus an allowance for improvements, adjustment for inflation, and possibly a small share of any equity increases. In some cities, LECs have been developed as part of a larger HOPE VI project. However, here we are concerned with the ways in which LECs, developed separately from HOPE VI projects, can address many of the negative impacts of HOPE VI. In this context, LECs can help to:

- **Preserve Affordable Housing.** Developing an LEC does not require the demolition of existing housing or the loss of public housing units. Rather, existing private or public housing can be converted into a limited-equity cooperative or LECs can be constructed through new development. LECs have been used successfully in Washington D.C. and Chicago to preserve affordable housing in neighborhoods experiencing gentrification. The LEC model emphasizes long-term affordability at both the unit-level (through resale restrictions) and at the building level (through covenants prohibiting the sale of the building to private developers).

- **Prevent the Displacement of Low-Income Residents.** In cities like Washington D.C., LECs have been used as a tool to avoid the displacement of low- and moderate-income residents when the owners of private apartment buildings seek to sell their properties. Unlike HOPE VI projects, which require residents to temporarily or permanently relocate as new housing is constructed, tenants usually can maintain their residence in their unit during their property's conversion to an LEC. This allows residents to maintain connections to neighbors and community institutions while gaining more control over the quality and management of their housing.

- **Allow Residents to Control the Management of their Housing.** While low-income residents often have little say in the development and implementation of HOPE VI projects, in the LEC model, residents own a share of the cooperative and are responsible for its governance and management. Sponsors of LEC development often provide training and technical assistance services to help residents develop skills in governance, contracting, and financial management.

Some have critiqued LECs for the restrictions they place on residents' ability to gain the full equity of their property at resale. While LEC residents do not gain the same wealth-building opportunities they would have as homeowners, they do have access to secondary mortgages, tax deductions, and lower purchase prices and monthly payments that can lead to increased savings. A review of two LECs – one in California and one in Georgia – found that median rates of return to resellers were 6.5 percent and 14.1 percent, respectively. In the latter case, this was a higher rate of return than owners would have realized had they invested their down payment in the stock or bond market. In interviews and focus groups, LEC residents also express high levels of satisfaction with their housing.

LECs also play an important neighborhood-level role in stabilizing communities during periods of disinvestment and gentrification. A study of limited-equity cooperatives in Washington D.C. found that the majority of LECs that had been established in the District over a 25-year period remained in operation during that period, with only 4 out of 81 properties experiencing foreclosure. A review of seven shared-equity housing projects found that the two LECs included in the sample had not experienced a single foreclosure during the life of the programs.

Beyond the economic benefits that they provide to individuals and communities, LECs provide important social benefits to residents. Studies have shown that residents increase their social capital and civic engagement as a result of participating in an LEC, where they are required to work with other residents to maintain and improve their building. These studies also have found that higher levels of social capital present in LEC buildings translate into lower crime rates and higher quality housing, compared to other government and privately-owned housing.

LECs have provided a successful model for developing and preserving low-cost housing since the turn of the 20th century. Over time, several different models for creating and sustaining LECs have developed across the country, with the support of state and federal legislation.

- **Local Incentives for LEC Development in New York City:** The first housing cooperatives in the U.S. were constructed in New York City, which is now home to the largest number of LECs in the country. Cooperatives in New York City initially were established by labor unions and immigrant associations to provide members with low-cost housing. The New York Housing Act of 1927 supported the construction of cooperatives, providing a 50-year tax exemption on any increases in cooperatives' property values. In 1955, the state legislature enacted the Mitchell-Lama program, which provided low-interest loans and property tax exemptions to developers of cooperative housing for low- and moderate-income residents. This legislation resulted in the construction of 60,000 LEC units in the 1950s and 1960s. Two decades later, the state established the Tenant Interim Lease Program and the Community Management Program to enable tenants to assume ownership of foreclosed properties. Along with ownership rights, tenants receive management training and funding for repairs. As of 2003, 795 buildings, with 16,692 units, had been converted to LECs through this process.

- **Washington D.C.'s "Right of First Refusal" Law:** In response to increasing gentrification in low-income neighborhoods, the City Council of DC enacted a "right of first refusal" law in 1977, providing tenants with the first right to purchase their apartment building if it was placed on the market. The District government also provides subsidized financing to help residents buy their building. Long-term affordability is maintained by allowing residents who sell their unit to receive their initial down payment plus interest, rather than the full market value of the unit. However, DC does not prohibit the resale of cooperatives to private developers; residents can collectively decide to dissolve their cooperative and sell their building, subject to the conditions of their financing. In spite of this option, most residents have chosen to maintain their LECs: only 18 percent of DC LECs were sold or converted to condominiums from 1977 to 2001.

- **Federal Mortgage Assistance and Long-Term Affordability Covenants in Chicago:** Many limited-equity cooperatives were developed in Chicago with assistance from federal mortgage insurance and low-income housing preservation programs. For example, Chicago's Hermitage Manor Cooperative was built in 1969 using a federally-insured mortgage through the National Housing Act on land that had been cleared as part of an urban renewal effort. The cooperative includes 108 townhomes in 17 buildings and has been resident-owned and operated since 1971. Long-term affordability was initially maintained through federal mortgage guidelines that prohibited residents from selling the cooperative during the life of the 40-year loan. After the loan had been paid, residents adopted a covenant to maintain the cooperative's structure and affordability.

- **Conversion of Manufactured Housing to LECs in Rural Areas:** While LECs often are associated with inner-city housing development, the model also has expanded to rural communities. Since 1984, 72 mobile home parks have been converted to limited-equity cooperatives in New Hampshire, and this effort currently is being replicated across the country. In New Hampshire, a cooperative housing corporation purchased the mobile home park's land, improved the infrastructure, and continues to maintain the park. Mobile home residents own their homes, lease their lots from the cooperative, and collectively own the cooperative as shareholders. They receive training and technical assistance on establishing and managing a cooperative from the Manufactured Housing Park Program, and receive financing from local banks and the New Hampshire Community Loan Fund (NHCLF). Long-term affordability is maintained by a state law requiring all cooperatives that dissolve to transfer their assets to another cooperative or nonprofit. However, no restrictions are placed on the resale price of homes, under the assumption that housing prices will remain affordable once the land has been purchased and the rents have been stabilized.

Developing a limited-equity cooperative often requires partnerships between, public, private, and nonprofit institutions. As the models above demonstrate, financing for the construction or rehabilitation of LEC buildings often is provided with loans from both private and public institutions. Local governments often contract with nonprofit organizations to manage the construction and rehabilitation of buildings, provide land (as in the case of community land trusts), and offer training and technical assistance for residents. State and local governments, in cooperation with other entities, can support the implementation of LECs by:

- **Facilitating the Construction or the Conversion of Units to LECs:** There are many ways that policymakers, in partnership with private developers, nonprofits, and financial institutions, can support the construction of new LECs or the conversion of existing buildings to LECs. States or localities that have adopted inclusionary zoning policies can include provisions for LECs as part of new construction. Inclusionary zoning policies mandate that a percentage of new housing construction be made affordable to lower-income households. Policymakers can partner with nonprofit community land trusts to develop LECs on land leased from the trust. State and local governments also can provide funding, through housing production trust funds or other sources, to nonprofits to develop new LECs or convert existing housing stock to a limited-equity cooperative. Often states and local governments have enacted laws that can make it challenging to develop or finance LECs. Policymakers can modify this legislation as well as increase opportunities for LEC conversion by adopting a "right of first refusal" law, allowing existing tenants the first opportunity to purchase their property if it is placed on the market or under foreclosure.

- **Ensuring the Long-Term Affordability of LEC Units:** LECs traditionally have relied on two mechanisms to preserve their long-term affordability. The first is a limit on the equity that individuals can realize when they sell their unit in an LEC. The second is a limit on the ability of LEC members to sell their building to private developers. Many local governments have implemented these deed and resale restrictions without the assistance of state laws. However, some states such as Maine and Oregon have passed laws explicitly permitting the development of affordable housing covenants and other restrictions to protect LECs from legal challenges. For LECs that are developed with federally-funded mortgages, policymakers can establish deed covenants to ensure that affordability is maintained after the loan is paid off and federal restrictions no longer apply.

- **Assisting with Management Training and Capacity-Building for LEC Residents:** The LEC model provides an opportunity for low-income residents not only to own their unit but to participate in the governance and management of the larger housing cooperative. However, in order to be successful, this model requires that residents have the time and technical expertise to lead or attend board meetings, set rules to govern the use and disposition of housing units, manage finances, and supervise contractors, among other responsibilities. State and local governments can provide training and technical assistance directly, as part of their administration of LECs, or can partner with a nonprofit to provide services. For example, in New York City, the local government contracts with the nonprofit Urban Homesteading Assistance Network to provide free training and technical assistance to LEC residents.

In the wake of the housing crisis and economic downturn, policies that provide affordable housing and stabilize communities are critical to the well-being of American families. Policymakers at the local and state level have tended to adopt a HOPE-VI model as their primary form of affordable housing preservation with an emphasis on demolishing existing public housing. The current economic recovery provides an opportunity for local and state governments to pursue a different approach, one that would improve the infrastructure of existing public housing, allowing residents to build wealth, maintain neighborhood ties, and stabilize neighborhoods.

KEY RESOURCES

Alexander, Lisa T. 2009. "Stakeholder Participation in New Governance: Lessons from Chicago's Public Housing Reform Experiment." *Georgetown Journal on Poverty Law Policy* 16:2.

Center for Nonprofit Housing and Economic Development. 2002. "A Study of Limited-Equity
Cooperatives in the District of Columbia." http://www.cnhed.org/shared/layouts/newsletter. jsp?_event=view&_id=12013o_c_sU127242_s_i170033.

Barnds, Ann, Martha Glas, Matthew Glesne, Claudia Saravia, Patricia A. Wright, and Yittayih Zelalem. 2004. "Affordable Housing Cooperatives: Conditions and Prospects in Chicago." Nathalie P. Voorhees Center for Neighborhood and Community Improvement, University of Illinois at Chicago. http://www.uic.edu/cuppa/voorheesctr/Publications/Affordable %20 Cooperative%20Housing%2004.pdf.

Davis, John Emmeus. 2006. "Shared Equity Homeownership: The Changing Landscape of Resale-Restricted, Owner-Occupied Housing." National Housing Institute. http://burlingtonassociates.com/resources/archives/SharedEquity Home.pdf.

Goetz, Edward G. 2003. *Clearing the Way: Deconcentrating the Poor in Urban America*. Washington, D.C.: Urban Institute Press.

Goetz, Edward G. 2011. "Where Have All the Towers Gone? The Dismantling of Public Housing in US Cities." *Journal of Urban Affairs* 33(3):267-287

Goetz, Edward G. and Karen Chapple. 2010. "'You Gotta Move': Advancing the Debate on the Record of Dispersal. " *Housing Policy Debate* 20(2):1-28.

Saegert, Susan and Lymari Benitez. 2005. "Limited Equity Housing Cooperatives: Defining a Niche in the Low-Income Housing Market." *Journal of Planning Literature* 19: 427-439.

Sazama, Gerald W. 2000. "Lessons from the History of Affordable Housing Cooperatives in the United States: A Case Study in American Affordable Housing Policy." *American Journal of Economics and Sociology* 59(4): 573-608.

Sazama, Gerald and Roger Wilcox. 1995. "An Evaluation of Limited Equity Housing Cooperatives in the United States." University of Connecticut Department of Economics Working Paper Series, 1995-02.

Sherrif, Ryan. 2010. "Shared Equity Homeownership State Policy Review." Center for Housing Policy. http://www.nhc.org/media/documents/State_Policy_Inventory_ Report.pdf?phpMyAdmin=d3a4afe4e37aae985c684e22d8f65929.

Small, Mario L. and Monica McDermott. 2006. "The Presence of Organizational Resources in Poor Urban Neighborhoods: An Analysis of Average and Contextual Effects." *Social Forces* 84(3):1697-1724.

Small, Mario L. and Jessica Feldman. "Ethnographic Evidence, Heterogeneity, and Neighbourhood Effects after Moving to Opportunity." In *Neighborhood Effects Research: New Perspectives*, edited by M. van Hamm, D. Manley, N. Bailey, L. Simpson, and D. Maclennan. Dordrecht, Netherlands: Springer.

Temkin, Kenneth, Brett Theodos, and David Price. 2010. "Balancing Affordability and Opportunity: An Evaluation of Affordable Homeownership Programs with Long-term Affordability Controls, Cross-Site Report." The Urban Institute. http://www.urban.org/UploadedPDF/412244-balancing-affordabiliity.pdf.

ABOUT THE AUTHORS

John N. Robinson III is a doctoral student in the Department of Sociology and a Graduate Fellow in Legal Studies at Northwestern University. His research interests include law, public policy, organizations, and urban poverty. Using comparative-historical methods, his current work investigates the link between the poverty de-concentration model of housing policy and residential dispossession among urban poor households, paying special attention to the role of legal aid organizations and tenant associations as intervening variables. Previously, he has published in the *Qualitative Sociology Review, Media, Culture & Society*, and the *Western Journal of Black Studies*.

Katie Kerstetter is a doctoral student in the Public and Applied Sociology Program and a Research Assistant at the Center for Social Science Research at George Mason University. Her research employs qualitative and quantitative methods to examine issues related to poverty and inequality, education, and social policy. She recently was awarded funding from the Foundation for Community Association Research to examine barriers to tenant participation in community associations. Prior to attending GMU, Katie worked at the DC Fiscal Policy Institute, where her research and advocacy focused on collaborating with low-income women, advocates, and agency staff to improve services for D.C. welfare recipients.

CHAPTER 11

Societal Aging in the U.S.:
Impact on Health, Economic Security and Retirement

Chris Wellin, Ph.D.
Illinois State University

Brooke Hollister, Ph.D.
University of California, San Francisco

THE PROBLEM

Income and retirement security for older people, as well as for those with chronic illness or disability, are facing threats we haven't seen since the implementation of major welfare policies in the 1960s. These threats arise in the aftermath of economic recession and fiscal retrenchment at multiple levels of government; at a time when the society is demographically aging; and when the proportion of the most economically vulnerable sub-populations of older adults, single women and people of color, is expanding.

Despite widespread consensus regarding the prime causes of the current recession in the domain of political economy—including tax cuts throughout a decade of foreign wars, global economic recession and, in the U.S., reckless lending practices leading to a speculative bubble in the housing market and inflation of value in this key sector of the economy— the pain of the recession has fallen heavily on vulnerable people across the class spectrum, as documented by researchers Engemann and Wall, as well as Allegretto. This erosion of the *aged welfare state* (of which Social Security and Medicare are cornerstones) comes amidst demographic aging spurred by the maturation of approximately 70 million baby boomers, as well as significant increases in the segments of the older population that are most vulnerable to poverty in late life—single women, and ethnic and racial minorities. Moreover, proposals to reduce Social Security and Medicare benefits are especially dangerous at a time when both the availability and value of private pensions have eroded. Taken together, these trends foretell longer work careers, and economic distress for millions of older Americans who have, in good faith, contributed to entitlement policies for decades. While many older people are willing and able to work to supplement retirement income, research by Kenneth Lang and Yang Yang reveals that those with the greatest financial need tend to be less healthy, and more subject to chronic illness and disability. Thus, while major entitlement programs have not resolved persistent economic disparities within the older population, the need for such programs will only increase in the years to come.

Legitimate concerns about generational equity can obscure appreciation of the longer, life course trajectories and contributions of the older population. Now that the baby boomers are retiring, most after long socially and economically beneficial careers, many policy-makers imply that they are not deserving of the full benefits they have earned. The current focus on the retiree to worker ratio as the central problem, rather than the overall dependency ratio (working adults to children/retiree/disabled dependents) promotes intergenerational conflict and blatant ageism.

Understanding the historical context is essential; Social Security was created during the Great Depression, a time not so different from the current economic recession. Social Security and other New Deal programs enhanced elders' economic security, stimulated the economy, opened up jobs for younger adults and reduced the care-giving burden on working age adults. However the role of programs like these in supporting economic security are largely ignored in mainstream media and current political discourse about how to bolster the wavering economy. Without economic security, many older adults would once again return to the workforce or rely on family members and communities to support and care for them. Without economic security, older adults would be more reliant on welfare programs, crowd working age adults out of the workforce, and cease to be consumers in an economy sorely in need of increased consumption.

Alas, prospects for fair-minded, incremental policy responses to these challenges seem ever more remote as national political debates have devolved into divisions over long-term budget deficits and tax policy. The failure of a Congressional "super committee" to arrive at a compromise on deficit reduction portends across-the-board cuts to discretionary programs, even as unemployment and foreclosure rates remain high and states are implementing draconian cuts in social services.

THE RESEARCH EVIDENCE

Millions of middle-class, stably-employed workers, have seen their retirement assets (private pensions and savings) dramatically decrease in value. Ostensible safeguards of such assets, such as the Federal Government's *Pension Benefit Guaranty Corporation*, are woefully inadequate to provide such protections. The impact of this cascade of events, evident in rising rates of poverty and other indicators of income insecurity, is especially disruptive, coming as the eldest of the baby boomer cohorts are reaching their mid-60s. This demographic "bulge" coincides with an economic recession, potentially of global scale, and with polarization in the political process that is unprecedented in modern American history.

Demographic Trends

Persistent patterns of decreased birth and death rates in recent decades, in conjunction with the maturation of the large baby boomer cohorts of the post WWII period, have combined to accelerate societal aging in the U.S. At the turn of the twentieth century, fewer than 5 percent of Americans were over the age of 65; in the first decades of the twenty-first century, that proportion will approach 20 percent—a nearly five-fold increase. Within this grayer nation, the proportion of the "oldest old," aged 85 and over, is the fastest-growing segment of the older population. Presently numbering some 5.8 million Americans, this number is projected to more than triple by mid-century according to U.S. Census data. Inasmuch as there is a *compression of morbidity* or illness in the final years of life, with concomitant increases in health care costs at this stage of life, improvements in health status for elders as a group will only *partly* buffer the increased economic pressure on major entitlement programs—Social Security, Medicare, and Medicaid, the latter being the largest public funding source for long-term care.

Public Discourse and Social Construction of Fiscal Crisis

The cultural and media framings of these challenges, and the measures taken thus far to address them, have revealed the political economy of the U.S. in a harsh light. The massive federal "bailout" that spanned the Bush and Obama administrations, has protected the financial industry and corporate profits, even as unemployment and foreclosure rates in the U.S. have reached historically-high levels. John Williamson and Diane Watts-Roy have shown that media coverage often focuses on the rudimentary demographics and economics of social programs, e.g., worker to retiree ratios, 75-year projections of financial stability, and the annual percentage of GDP spent on social programs. They argue that worker to retiree ratios are often used to mislead audiences into believing that social programs are unsustainable with fewer workers financing more beneficiaries. However, when examining the *overall* dependency ratio—the ratio of children, retirees, and the disabled to working-age adults—we see that in fact it will be lower at the peak of the retirement of baby boomers than it was nearly a half-century ago when the baby boomers were younger.

Similarly, the aging of the population has led some politicians and pundits to fan the flames of *apocalyptic demography*, implying that the sheer numbers of elders represent a crushing burden on major entitlement programs. One hears repeated claims, for example, that the Social Security trust fund is "broke," despite the fact that (according to non-partisan projections) the fund is projected to deliver full, guaranteed benefits until 2037, and will continue to pay out 76 percent of benefits in the years to follow. Despite alarmist rhetoric about the solvency of the Social Security system, we know that incremental changes can be made that will preserve the system for decades to come. Indeed, some such changes, such as raising the level of income subject to Social Security taxes, would also bring greater progressivity to its funding.

Similarly, alarmist rhetoric regarding inflation in health care costs, centering on Medicare, often attributes the trend to societal aging. However, according to the Congressional Budget Office, while there will be cost increases associated with the spike in the number of beneficiaries, the continued rise in Medicare costs will have more to do with *general* health care inflation due largely to costs associated with the development and utilization of new medical technologies. Ironically, however, one of the greatest areas of need in U.S. health care policy is *not* in curative techno-medicine, but rather in relatively low-cost, low-tech aspects of preventative, home and community-based care for the chronically ill.

Poverty in the Older Population

Beginning with the passage of the Social Security Act in 1935, according to sociologist Beth A. Rubin, a social contract or *labor-capital accord* was struck with American retirees. The funding reconciled the goals of structuring Social Security as an earned entitlement—with benefits tied to paid work and indexed to earnings—while also achieving modest redistribution of wealth in order to provide a modicum of economic security to the lowest wage earners. Three decades later, with the passage of Medicare, the country took another major step toward ensuring economic security for retirees.

The positive impact of these programs is not in dispute: according to a brief by the *Center for American Progress,* between 1959 and 1974, the overall poverty rate among older Americans fell from 35 to 15 percent. Incremental changes in Social Security, including cost of living adjustments and elimination of the "income penalty" for beneficiaries (by which they had been penalized, dollar for dollar, for post-retirement earnings) led to continued decreases in poverty rates among older people. By 2006, overall elderly poverty rates fell to roughly 9 percent, though substantial disparities continue within sub-groups of older people. Over 2.3 million women over age 65 are poor, which is roughly twice the number of older men who are poor by this standard. Nearly 20 percent of women who are single, divorced, or widowed are poor, and their risk of poverty increases with age. Women over the age of 75 are more than three times as likely to be poor as their male counterparts, an alarming finding in light of the fact that, as our society ages, the greatest growth of the older population is among those 85 years and older. Current analyses *underestimate* poverty by failing to include out of pocket medical expenses. It is past-due for the Census Bureau to have revised the formula. Preliminary estimates are that the aged poverty rate of roughly 9 percent will double, once medical expenses are deducted from income.

As the U.S. population becomes older, it is also becoming more ethnically and racially diverse. Unfortunately, the legacy of inequalities in education, earnings, pensions and health insurance will exacerbate what have been persistent inequalities in these expanding communities as they age. We know, for example, that income disparities between non-Hispanic whites and people of color are substantial and that the latter are significantly less likely than whites to have pensions that supplement Social Security benefits. In addition, the disparities in income are modest in comparison with the gap in wealth; according to 2009 data calculated by Rakesh Kochhar and colleagues, the median net worth of white households was twenty times that for blacks.

In turning our attention to the most economically vulnerable in the class spectrum (single women, ethnic/racial minority members, and disabled workers), many of whom have labored in the service or informal economies and thereby lacked employment benefits or adequate wages/salaries, the risks and adversity are especially stark. Federal austerity, combined with deficits in many state governments, is leading to draconian cuts in Medicaid funding and the extensive network of health and social service programs reliant on such funding sources.

Lastly, the tendency to use a "unified budget" rather than a budget depicting the federal fund (exclusive of trust funds which are financed by payroll taxes and earmarked to support Social Security and Medicare) obscures the federal budget and drivers of the federal deficit. By including the expenses of Social Security and Medicare in descriptions of the budget and as a percentage of necessary spending, without acknowledging that it is fully funded, not only distracts from the proportion of spending on the military but also subjects these fully funded programs to attacks on spending in the name of reducing the deficit. Social Security and Medicare add not a dime to the federal deficit. Yet, the National Commission on Fiscal Responsibility and Reform published a report advocating several changes to the Social Security Program including reducing cost-of living adjustments (COLAs), raising the retirement age, and changing the benefit formula. These same proposals were made by members of the United States Congress Joint Select Committee on Deficit Reduction (the "super committee"). As a result of partisan politics, the super committee failed to agree to a plan that would avert automatic cuts to both defense and discretionary funding (Medicare benefits, Medicaid, and Social Security are exempt from cuts) in 2013.

RECOMMENDATIONS AND SOLUTIONS

"A nation's greatness is measured by how it treats its weakest members."
Mahatma Gandhi

In order to evolve into a more just society, we must be able to preserve the existing tools of economic and social justice, reframe the ways in which social and economic justice are perceived and measured, and proactively pursue an overall social justice agenda. The fight for social justice for the elderly and people with disabilities will commence in the cultural, economic, and political arenas. The effective use of Internet and communication technologies (ICT) is necessary to effect change.

Organizational bureaucracy, competition for funding, and proprietary claims on intellectual capital, often work against the interests of organizations, individuals, and policy makers. The challenge facing social and economic justice advocacy groups is the need to join forces and be pro-active rather than separatist and reactive. For example, the *Strengthen Social Security* Campaign is comprised of nearly 300 national and state organizations representing more than 50 million Americans from many of the nation's leading aging, labor, disability, women's, children, consumer, civil rights and equality organizations. The coalition has bridged many issues that, traditionally, have prevented coalitions from succeeding. They have quickly become the resource for mainstream media on Social Security and are called upon for expert testimony, interviews, and speeches.

The efficiency of new ICTs facilitates access to the cultural, economic, and political arenas in which a social justice agenda can potentially be fulfilled. Mark Surman and Katherine Reilly argue that the issue of "…using networked technologies strategically, politically, creatively – is amongst the most pressing that civil society faces in the information society". Online informational campaigns combined with petition gathering and letter writing has facilitated the democratic participation of previously disenfranchised groups. Effective use of technology can fuel social change and help to overcome many cultural, monetary, and political barriers to progress.

Changing Hearts and Minds

The following recommendations assume the existence of free discussion of issues and equal access to free and accurate information and technology. Supporters of a social justice agenda, with respect to health, economic security, and retirement in an aging U.S. find consensus on the need to:

- **Combat ageism.** Ageism against the old includes prejudicial attitudes towards older people, old age, and the aging process; discriminatory practices against older people; and institutional practices and policies that perpetuate stereotypes about older people. An economically and socially just society regards older adults as individuals who have earned their benefits, contribute to society, and are worthy of respect and a life of dignity and security. Ideally, tens of millions of retired Americans with the time and commitment to serve their communities should be celebrated as a deep resource. Unfortunately, our society has used stereotypes to construct a climate of crisis around age and *dependency* through concepts like apocalyptic demography, the silver tsunami, greedy geezers, intergenerational equity, unsustainable worker to retiree ratios, 75-year solvency projections, and demagogic warnings about the bankruptcy of Social Security and Medicare.

- **Require public education about Social Security and Medicare.** Education about social insurance programs is essential to maintain support and build a populace devoted to social and economic justice. Social insurance programs need to be reconceived as social goods benefitting all Americans, not just those currently receiving benefits. Coalitions like Strengthen Social Security and organizations like the Gray Panthers and the National Committee to Preserve Social Security and Medicare are on the front lines of these efforts. These efforts will help sustain high levels of public support for such policies.

- **Improve access to, accountability in, and validity of mainstream *and* alternative media**. An initial step to changing public perception of aging and social and economic justice is to expand and monitor the use of alternative media as a trusted source of information. Online news and blogs have created a venue for voices kept out of mainstream media, and social media has created an increasingly smaller world where information can be shared across geographic, cultural, and socioeconomic divides. Social and alternative media have enabled movements to operate outside of the standard political, economic, and cultural arenas of power that have previously barred their access to the social collective conscious.

People Over Profit

Without campaign finance reform, more stringent financial regulations, and increased accountability in the finance sector, the pursuit of profit will continue at the expense of some of our most vulnerable citizens. The recent Supreme Court Decision on *Citizens United v. Federal Election Commission* may have further eroded the voice of the citizenry in elections, by eliminating restrictions on campaign spending by corporations and unions.

- **Re-evaluate and implement a measure of poverty reflective of economic security.** Economic justice entails the right of all citizens to live with dignity and with an income that meets basic necessities. Our current measure of poverty, the Federal Poverty Level (FPL), was developed in 1964 and was calculated using only the cost of food, estimated to be one-third of an individual's budget. Economic security today requires enough money to be able to pay for rent, food, childcare, health care, transportation, and taxes. Institutionalizing an updated measure of poverty will ensure people in need can access programs like Medicaid, Supplemental Security Income (SSI), Food Stamps, and the Children's Health Insurance Program (CHIP). We welcome the revision of the decades-old Federal Poverty Measure adopted in 2012 by the Department of Health and Human Services.

- **Allow caregiving credits in the eligibility criteria for Social Security and Medicare.** Much of our necessary caregiving work is unacknowledged and uncompensated. The years spent raising children and caring for loved ones do not qualify an individual for Social Security and Medicare. A just society needs to recognize the value of caregiving and support caregivers in their role in order to avoid costly and unnecessary hospitalization and institutionalization. Furthermore, even as their labor force participation approaches parity with those of men, caregiving responsibilities seriously undermine both the continuity and career trajectories of women's employment.

- **Expand the use of *quality of life* measures in business and politics.** Today's economic environment overvalues returns on investment and virtually ignores quality of life. This narrow focus on monetary value and growth neglects the potential social harm of many capitalist endeavors. While economic growth can lead to a higher quality of life, the two are not synonymous and improving quality of life needs to be the ultimate goal of all economic activities. Quality of life measures need to be used in tandem with other measures of social and economic progress.

Proactive Politics

Given the partisan politics ruling Washington, DC today, the proactive participation of citizens and advocacy organizations is crucial to achieve any progress on social and economic justice issues. The following recommendations are proactive and feasible solutions that will improve the economic and social justice of older adults and their families. However, without improved accountability in politics, the restoration of the budget process, and the examination of the political processes that promote partisan politics, these changes will not be possible.

- **Reform the health care system to meet the needs of people.**
  Although imperfect, the Affordable Care Act of 2010 (ACA) represents a step in the right direction. A centrist approach, which preserves the central role of private insurers, this policy had its origins in bi-partisan proposals developed over many years. We can build upon the structure established by this reform, claim successes where they are found, and expand the cost-saving mechanisms that will enable the health care system to affordably and effectively treat all people. If the health care exchanges fail to provide quality affordable health care and help control costs in the overall health care system, a public option must be made available. If the public option fails to provide quality and affordable health care that can slow health care spending, a single payer health care system is the solution. We are the only industrialized nation without universal coverage, we spend more than any other nation on health care costs, and yet our health care system is ranked 37th in the world by the World Health Organization. Better models have been proven to work elsewhere and if the ACA won't deliver the healthcare system we deserve, it's time to change our approach.

- **Create policies to control the costs of in-home health care and long-term care.** One example would be to reinstate and make mandatory the Community Living Assistance Services and Supports Program (CLASS). The unmanageable costs of the CLASS program that led it to be abandoned were the result of the optional nature of contributions. Without a mandatory, social insurance approach, only the sickest people will contribute to and benefit from the program. If CLASS was mandatory, individual premiums for long-term care (LTC) insurance would be modest, Medicaid spending on LTC would decrease, nursing home costs would be controlled, and community living and in-home supportive services can be expanded. A LTC social insurance program would allow people to remain in their homes and in their communities decreasing costs while prioritizing patient preference rather than nursing home profits.

- **Strengthen and expand existing Medicare and Social Security systems.** Both Social Security and Medicare can be strengthened and expanded to offer better economic and health security. Many of the feasible policy options will benefit the economy, by ensuring that beneficiaries can continue to act as consumers and maintain their health independence, avoiding high institutional costs without burdening family members or loved ones. Improving these programs can also decrease the need to provide support to inefficient or failing programs like Medicaid's LTC funding and the Children's Health Insurance Program. The following options are stand-alone policies that could be passed independently and not as a bargaining chip in larger political negotiations. These are solutions that are cost effective, feasible, and practical.

- **Other policy recommendations Vis-a-Vis Medicare:**
  - Decrease the 2-year waiting period for Disability benefits.
  - Create a Medicare operated prescription drug plan that can negotiate prices.
  - Allow drug importation / re-importation.
  - Improve preventative health services.
  - Create formularies and coverage guidelines.

- Expand Medicare to cover community-based long-term services and supports.
- Support, educate, and provide respite services to informal caregivers.
- Establish mental health parity.
- Improve and expand hospice and palliative care options.
- Expand Medicare to cover an increasing portion of the population.

- **Strengthening Social Security:**
  - Raise the cap on taxable income or lift the cap completely.
  - Include state and federal workers.
  - Decrease the 2-year waiting period for disability benefits.
  - Implement a care giving credit for informal caregivers.
    Recent campaigns to preserve and protect Social Security and

Medicare have relied upon simple messaging, inter-organizational collaboration, and appealing to the social values of family, community, and solidarity. These campaigns have been strengthened by the realities of living in a period of economic recession, increased influence of lobbying and corporate influence in the political process, partisan "gridlock," and a growing disenchantment over the status quo. However, in addition to defending programs, fighting bad policy, and refuting myths, the movement toward a more just society in an aging U.S. must be proactive in messaging, advocacy, cross-generational coalitions, and politics.

KEY RESOURCES

Allegretto, Sylvia A. 2011. "The State of Working America's Wealth: Through Volatility and Turmoil, the Gap Widens. *Economic Policy Institute Briefing Paper 392*. Retrieved April 12, 2012 (http://www.epi.org/publications/entry/the_state_of_working_a mericas_wealth_2011).

Cawthorne, Alexandra. 2008. Elderly Poverty: The Challenge Before Us. *Center for American Progress*. Retrieved April 12, 2012 (http://www.americanprogress.org/issues/2008/07/elderly_pover ty.html).

Cook, Fay L. and Meredith B. Czaplewski. 2009. "Public Opinion and

Social Insurance: The American Experience" Pp. 251-278 in *Social Insurance and Social Justice: Social Security, Medicare, and the Campaign Against Entitlements,* edited by L. Rogne, C. Estes, B. Grossman, B. Hollister, and E. Solway. New York: Springer Publishing Company.

Domhoff, G. William. 1987. "Corporate-Liberal Theory and the Social Security Act: A Chapter in the Sociology of Knowledge." *Politics and Society,* 15(3): 297-330.

Engemann, Kristie M. and Howard J. Wall. 2009. "The Effects of Recessions Across Demographic Groups." *Federal Reserve Bank of St. Louis,* Working Paper 2009-052A, October. Retrieved April 12, 2012 (http://research.stlouisfed.org/wp/2009/2009-052.pdf).

Estes, Carroll L. 2001. *Social Policy and Aging: A Critical Perspective.* Thousand Oaks, CA: SAGE.

Hudson, Robert B. 2010. "Contemporary Challenges to Aging Policy." Pp. 3-20 in *The New Politics of Old Age Policy (2nd Ed.),* edited by R. B. Hudson Baltimore, MD: The Johns Hopkins University Press.

Kochhar, Rakesh, Richard Fry and Paul Taylor. 2011. "Wealth Gaps Rise to Record Highs Between Whites, Blacks and Hispanics." *Pew Research Center,* July 26. Retrieved April 12, 2012 (http://www.pewsocialtrends.org/2011/07/26/wealth-gaps-rise-to-record-highs-between-whites-blacks-hispanics/).

Land, Kenneth C. and Yang Yang. 2006. "Morbidity, Disability, and Mortality." Pp. 41-58 in *Handbook of Aging and the Social Sciences (6th Ed.),* edited by R. H. Binstock and L. K. George. New York: Academic Press.

National Commission on Fiscal Responsibility and Reform. 2010. "The Moment of Truth," Washington, DC: The White House, December. Retrieved (http://www.fiscalcommission.gov/sites/fiscalcommission.gov/files/documents/TheMomentofTruth12_1_2010.pdf).

Quadagno, Jill. 2011. *Aging and the Life Course.* 5th Ed. New York, NY: McGraw-Hill.

Riley, Matilda W. and Riley, John W. 1994. "Age-integration and the Lives of Older People." *The Gerontologist,* 34(1): 110-115.

Rubin, Beth A. 1996. *Shifts in the Social Contract.* Thousand Oaks, CA: Pine Forge.

Surman, Mark and Katherine Reilly. 2003. "Appropriating the Internet for Social Change: Toward the Strategic Use of Networked Technologies by Transnational civil Society Organizations," *Social Science Research Council,* November. Retrieved (http://ict4peace.org/pubs/Appropriating%20the%20Internet%20for%20Social%20Change.pdf).

Vincent, Grayson K. and Victoria A. Velkoff. 2010, "The Next Four

Decades: The Older Population in the United States 2010 to 2050."
Census Bureau Current Population Reports #P25-1138, May.

WHO. 2000. "The World Health Report 2000: Health Systems: Improving
Performance," Geneva, Switzerland: World Health Organization.
Retrieved
(http://www.who.int/entity/whr/2000/en/whr00_en.pdf).

Williamson, John B., Watts-Roy, Diane M. 2009. "Aging Boomers,
Generational Equity, and Framing the Debate Over Social
Security." Pp. 153-169 in *Boomer Bust? Economic and Political Issues of
the Graying Society*, edited by R.B. Hudson. Westport, CT:
Greenwood Publishing.

ABOUT THE AUTHORS

Chris Wellin (Ph.D. Northwestern University) is an Assistant Professor of
Sociology in the Department of Sociology and Anthropology at Illinois
State University, and Coordinator of Gerontology Programs. He is a
sociologist whose teaching and research interests focus on critical
gerontology, the study of work and occupations, and
qualitative/interpretive research methods. His publications have appeared
in such outlets as *Current Research on Occupations and Professions; Teaching
Sociology; Qualitative Sociology; Journal of Aging and Social Policy*; and the
Handbook of Ethnography. A recent (2007) report summarizing ethnographic
research on paid care-giving was commissioned by a committee of the
National Academy of Sciences.

Brooke Hollister (Ph.D. University of California, San Francisco) is an
Assistant Professor of Sociology in the Department of Social and
Behavioral Sciences at the University of California, San Francisco. Her
teaching and research at the Institute for Health and Aging, at the
University of California, San Francisco focuses on aging health and social
policy issues. Dr. Hollister has testified before state legislature, and
presented at national professional conferences, and press conferences with
advocacy organizations (Gray Panthers, California Association of Retired
Americans, Senior Action Network, and AARP) and legislators (Nancy
Pelosi, Barbara Boxer, Lynn Woolsey, Susan Davis, and Jim Beall). Dr.
Hollister also serves as Vice Chair on the National Board of the Gray
Panthers, and has been a member since 2004.

AFTERWORD

We are approaching a dangerous point of no return for solving several social, political, economic, and environmental problems at the national and global level. The multiple crises of the Great Recession, rapid climate change, increasing economic inequality and growing poverty, a flawed and punitive immigration policy, lack of affordable health care and housing, as well as persistent and institutionalized racism, sexism and ageism, among others, leaves many with the feeling that our problems are insurmountable. Many polls show citizens' unease with the future, and frustration with the divisiveness of political rhetoric and the gridlock of Washington policy-making. At the same time there seems to be growing anger around bipartisan decisions that go against the grain of public desire, and in favor of social justice. More and more people are demanding accountability from political leaders and transnational corporations, as well as turning to local solutions to build alternative and socially just organizations and institutions.

Listening to the wisdom of social scientists in these times is crucial for working our way through the political morass. Sociologists in particular have much to offer regarding a concrete way forward that will counter many troubling trends. The authors in this volume have summarized the latest and best research in the field and articulated visionary yet practical solutions. What is assumed to be "common sense" on contentious political issues is frequently proven wrong by sociological research that analyzes how the implementation of social policies affects the people, organizations, and institutions that are most impacted. Sociological research on the ground needs to inform public policy decisions that impact inequality.

It is not only what government policies and programs do that is important, but also how it is done that matters, including understanding what is concealed by official reports. As Frances Fox Piven indicates in this volume (p. 82), "The official numbers…don't tell the full story." For example, Carolyn and Robert Perrucci report that many unemployed are not counted in government statistics and the unemployment rate for young, urban blacks is twice that of young whites in many areas. Policy decisions need to be based on scientific evidence and not just political expediency. A one-size-fits-all approach that ignores the intersecting realities of racial, gender, and class inequalities will not only reproduce existing social inequalities, but will also exacerbate them. Governance decisions need to mesh the short-term realities with long-term designs that transform systems for sustainable and effective results.

Collectively, the authors of this 2012 *Agenda for Social Justice* call for solutions that will build the material, social, and regulatory infrastructures for affordable housing and healthcare, jobs providing a living wage, creative paths to full citizenship, and the development of a greener, sustainable, and more equitable economy guided by communities rather than transnational corporations. These sociologists show how policy makers and all concerned citizens can nurture the public good, protect the commons, and create social justice for all. Rather than there being little that can be done, there is indeed so much that can and must be done.

We are at a tipping point in our society, one that will determine the kind of future we create. On the one side, are social forces pushing for retrenchment from the equality gains made by the social programs of "The Great Society," not to mention further gains acquired by the pressure of various social movements of the last five decades. On the other side, are social forces working towards building a better world where freedom, liberty, and justice for all exists not just in words but also in the lives of individuals and social groups who have struggled for so long to have an equitable part of the "American Dream," human rights, and dignity that all people deserve. The editors and authors of this *Agenda for Social Justice: Solutions 2012*, hope it will enlighten, inspire and motivate policy makers, academics, and concerned citizens to address social problems and to work towards bringing about a culture that continually delivers effective systems of social justice.

Brian Klocke, Ph.D.

State University of New York, Plattsburgh

SSSP Justice 21 Committee Member

ENDNOTES

[i] The full text of Dr. Perrucci's SSSP Presidential Address is available as follows: Perrucci, Robert. 2001. "Inventing Social Justice: SSSP and the Twenty-First Century." *Social Problems* 48(2): 159-167.

[ii] References supporting Cecilia Menjívar's chapter:

Abrego, Leisy J. 2011. "Legal Consciousness of Undocumented Latinos: Fear and Stigma as Barriers to Claims Making for First and 1.5 Generation Immigrants." *Law & Society Review* 45(2):337-69.

Brabeck, Kalina and Qingwen Xu. 2010. "The Impact of Detention and Deportation on Latino Immigrant Children and Families: A Quantitative Exploration." *Hispanic Journal of Behavioral Sciences*, 32(3): 341-361

Chavez, Leo. 2001. *The Latino Threat: Constructing Immigrants, Citizens, and the Nation.* Stanford: Stanford University Press.

De Genova, Nicholas. 2002. "Migrant "Illegality" and Deportability in Everyday Life." *Annual Review of Anthropology*, 31: 419-447.

Donato, Katharine M., and Amada Armenta. 2011. "What We Know About Unauthorized Migration." *Annual Review of Sociology* 37(1):25.1-25.15.

Gindling, T.H. and Sara Z. Poggio. 2008. Family Separation and Reunification as a Factor in the Educational Success of Immigrant Children. Maryland Institute for Policy Analysis and Research, University of Maryland. http://www.umbc.edu/economics/wpapers/wp_09_104_FinalReport-FamilySeparationandReunification.pdf.

Gonzales, Roberto G. "Learning to Be Illegal: Undocumented Youth and Shifting Legal Contexts in the Transition to Adulthood." *American Sociological Review*, 76 (4): 602-619.

Hagan, Jacqueline, Karl Eschbach, and Nestor Rodriguez. 2008. "U.S. Deportation Policy, Family Separation, and Circular Migration." *International Migration Review*, 42: 64-88.

Hagan, Jacqueline, Nestor Rodriguez, and Brianna Castro. 2011. "Social effects of mass deportations by the United States government, 2000-10." *Ethnic and Racial Studies* 34(8):1374-91.

Kanstroom, Daniel. 2007. *Deportation Nation: Outsiders in American History.* Cambridge, Mass.: Harvard University Press.

Massey, Durand Malone. 2002. *Beyond Smoke and Mirrors: Mexican Immigration in an Era of Economic Integration.* New York: Russell Sage Foundation.

Menjívar, Cecilia. 2006. Liminal Legality: Salvadoran and Guatemalan Immigrants' Lives in the United States." *American Journal of Sociology*, 111 (4): 999-1037.

Menjívar, Cecilia and Leisy Abrego. 2012 (forthcoming). "Legal Violence: Immigration Law and the Lives of Central American Immigrants." *American Journal of Sociology*, 117 (5)

Menjívar, Cecilia and Leisy Abrego. 2009. "Parents and Children across Borders: Legal Instability and Intergenerational Relations in Guatemalan and

Salvadoran Families." Pp. 160-189 in *Across Generations: Immigrant Families in America*, edited by Nancy Foner. New York: New York University Press.

Migration Information Source. 2011. US in Focus. http://www.migrationinformation.org/USFocus/

Ngai, Mae. 2006. "How Grandma got legal." *Los Angeles Times*, May 16.

Ngai, Mae M. 2004. *Impossible Subjects: Illegal Aliens and the Making of Modern America*. Princeton, NJ: Princeton University Press.

Passel, Jeffrey and D'Vera Cohen. 2011. Unauthorized Immigrant Population: National and State Trends, 2010. Washington, DC: Pew Hispanic Center. http://www.pewhispanic.org/files/2011/12/Unauthorized-Characteristics.pdf

Philips, Scott, Jacqueline Hagan and Nestor Rodriguez. 2006. "Brutal Borders? Examining the Treatment of Deportees During Arrest and Detention." *Social Forces*, 85, 1: 93-109.

Suárez-Orozco, Carola, Hirokazu Yoshikawa, Robert T. Teranishi and Marcelo Suárez-Orozco. 2011. "Growing Up in the Shadows: The Developmental Implications of Unauthorized Status." *Harvard Educational Review*, 81 (3): 438-472.

Villalón, Roberta. 2010. *Violence against Latina Immigrants: Citizenship, Inequality, and Community*. New Jersey: Rutgers University Press.

[iii] References supporting Frances Fox Piven's chapter:

Greg Kaufmann, "US Poverty: Past, Present and Future, The Nation, March 22, 2001; Kathryn Ann Edwards, "Another look at poverty in the Great Recession," [http://www.epi.org/authors/bio/edwards_kathryn] January 5, 2011.

Isabel V. Sawhill, "An Update to "Simulating the Effect of the 'Great Recession' on Poverty," Brookings Institution, October 7, 2010.Steven Pressman and Robert H. Scott III, "Consumer debt and poverty measurement," Focus, University of Wisconsin-Madison, Summer 2010.Women's Legal Defense and Education Fund, "Reading Between the Lines: Women's Poverty in the United States, 2009, 395 Hudson Street, New York City.

LaDonna Pavetti, Danilo Trisi and Liz Schott, "TANF Responded Unevenly to Increase in Need During Downturn," Center on Budget and Policy Priorities, Washington D.C. January 25, 2011.

Legal Momentum, "Poverty Rates for Single Mothers are Higher in the U.S. than in Other High Income Countries, 395 Hudson Street, NYC 10014, June 2011.

Hope Yen, "Census shows 1 in 2 people are poor or low income," Associated Press, December 15, 2011.

Sheldon Danziger, "Budget Cuts as Welfare Reform, American Economic Review 73 (1983), 65.

New York Times, Editorial, March 25, 2011.

www.ingramcontent.com/pod-product-compliance
Lightning Source LLC
Chambersburg PA
CBHW051435280526
45785CB00003B/1292